Nuts and Bolts:
A Survival Guide
for Non-profit
Organizations

Nuts and Bolts: A Survival Guide for Non-profit Organizations

Charles M. Dobbs &
Robert J. Ligouri

To order additional copies of this book, contact:
Xlibris Corporation
1-888-795-4274
www.Xlibris.com
Orders@Xlibris.com
14500

Contents

SECTION II.

Nuts and Bolts—
"Getting the Dollars!"

SECTION II:

Nuts and Bolts:
Grant Writing—
"Getting the Dollars"

SECTION III:

Nuts and Bolts: The "Little" Things

Introduction

"Nuts and Bolts, A Survival Guide for Non-Profit Organizations is a manual written for the Non-Profit Executive and for members of the Non-Profit Board of Directors. Tough economic times can play havoc for even the best of missions. This manual is designed to offer concrete strategies to allow an organization to fight through the times of declining revenue. The "nuts and bolts" strategies outlined in the following chapters will enable the organization to develop action steps that will attack short-term problems, and build a solid foundation for the future.

The manual will be divided into three sections:

Section I—Nuts and Bolts—Critical Strategies for Non-Profit Success

Section II—Nuts and Bolts—"Getting the Dollars"

Section III—Nuts and Bolts—"Saying thank-you"

The Authors of this manual have a long and successful history in the non-profit sector. It includes a combined total of over thirty years experience in the non-profit sector. Combined, the authors have been responsible as administrators for attracting over fifty million dollars to non-organizations, businesses, or causes.

The Oxford Group Inc. welcomes the opportunity to provide consultative services to Non-Profit Organizations as they move to implement the strategies outlined in this manual.

SECTION I.

Nuts and Bolts— Critical Strategies for Non-Profit Success

"No One has a Monopoly

on Virtue"

A number of years ago, one of the authors sat next to a national leader of one of the top non-profit organizations in the world. Her organization had demonstrated remarkable growth and stability. It had expanded during tough economic times, and had expanded into impoverished countries throughout the world. During our dinner conversation the author asked why the organization had continued to grow while others withered and died. Her answer was very simple:

1. Our focus is simple and our priorities are shared.
2. Our mission is easily communicated.
3. We fulfill our mission.

But most of all—she said—we realize that in our world today **"No one has a monopoly on virtue"**. I thought about her answer and what it meant to my organization. From that point on our conversation had a remarkable effect on my leadership and the direction that we took as an organization. I think it important that I touch on each of her points:

"Our Focus is simple and our priorities are shared"

This is an internal statement that you and your leadership team must critically evaluate. So often during the good times, a non-profit organization grows. During that growth period, the organization often implements new programs and initiatives. Many of these programs and initiatives represent expansions of existing programs or services, and others are new, innovative and leading edge. That is wonderful during the good times, but with it come problems and challenges. An organization's focus and emphasis can become blurred both internally and externally. Priorities often become unclear or too many in number. Resource allocation becomes more difficult, and communication within the organization and with key stakeholders over time gradually diminishes. During good economic times, you and those to whom you provide services may not clearly see the negative effects, however as revenue declines, and the need to maintain an increasing flow of resources to the organization grows—the issues of focus, and priorities can and often will become fatal. A simple test for the organization should suffice. Ask each of your Board and staff to independently write down the focus of the organization (mission), and its priorities. Give them only a sentence or two— nothing too long and nothing too involved. In some cases you will see a great deal of similarity; but in others, as it comes to priorities and central message, you will often note a great disparity of opinion.

Nuts and Bolts Strategies:

• Conduct a survey of your staff, Board, and even key donors. Ask them to write down in order what they see as the top 8-10 priorities of the organization. Tabulate the results. Once tabulated, it is now time as a group to settle on an agreed to order of priorities. This can be a very difficult task, and one in which there is great turf protection and even emotion. It is also essential for the organization to simplify its mission and priorities.

• Ask each of the same groups to write down what they feel is the central message that must be communicated to both internal and external audiences. Together, develop a centralized mission statement or message.

• Evaluate each of the top 5 priorities. Where is your organization truly at with each one? If we say for example that "participation growth" is our number one priority—how are we doing? What are we doing, and how are resources being allocated? And consider limiting yourself perhaps only to those top 5 priorities; you cannot be too many things to too many clients.

• Develop action plans off of your evaluation, how are you going to do it, who is going to do it, what is the cost, and how are we going to measure success.

"Our mission is easily communicated"

As an organization grows, and priorities evolve over time, the central message often becomes clouded. Each person in the organization has different levels of interest, organizational knowledge, expertise, and commitment. The list is endless as to our differences. That is why it is critical for an organization to keep its mission and message simple and easily communicated. I have spent years meeting with non-profit organizations throughout the country. I can assure you that the ones that were in the most difficulty were those who had some of the most complex mission statements and cluttered messages. They suffered staff issues, lack of Board involvement, and often during difficult times, declining public support and of course the issue of declining revenue. It's hard for an organization to pull in the same direction if everyone is not clear in what direction he or she is pulling.

Nuts and Bolts Strategies:

- As a staff, and Board, carefully review the mission statement. Is it clear, concise, and relevant?

- Conduct a Board and key volunteer survey in regards to the organization's mission. What do they see it? Do they feel it is being met? What communications issues do they see? What suggestions on improvements would they offer?

- Evaluate your mission statement. Is it consistent to what your organization is about, and are you effective in communicating the message?

- It is a big step for an organization to identify its central message. Once that is identified you are well along the road. Step one would be a close review of all communication methods. Stationery, newsletters, volunteer sign-ups, etc . . . how can you change them to better communicate your central theme, or mission?

- Develop a marketing plan. If the staff does not have that ability, use your board, outside consultants, or even outside agencies. Often "outsiders" can offer a new perspective and strategies. Some ad agencies often will donate much of their work to a non-profit in need of a marketing support.

- Develop a marketing component to the budget. Many in the community understand the value of communicating the central mission of an organization. It is a good project to use to get outside funding.

- Survey your staff, board, and key volunteers as to not just their expertise, but also to their spouses, and friends. Make your need known to others, develop an in-kind needs list and communicate it. You may be surprised at the talent level that comes forward for you.

"We fulfill our mission"

Simple words, but so important—"we fulfill our mission". When one analyzes that statement the question must be asked—"do we truly do what we say we are going to do?" During tough economic times, it is an absolute must if you are to survive as an organization. You must be able to make your case to both your internal and external audiences. You must have a clear operational plan that takes the words off of the paper, and puts those words into targeted action. And you must have some kind of effective, annual evaluation to demonstrate that you are meeting the challenge and achieving your goals and thus accomplishing your priorities.

The following is a true example:

I was appointed the Executive Director of a non-profit organization. On my first day on the new job, I went through the desk drawers as I prepared to move into the office. In one drawer I found a folder. In this folder were past due bills (some dated as far back as six-months) that totaled over $20,000! I promptly called our Board President at the time, told him about the past due bills (he was shocked), and asked our current balance at his bank. It was approximately $12,000. Well, he said, we are technically insolvent. After I hung up, I continued my "search" through the desk. In the next drawer I found our organization's strategic plan. It was bound, and one of the best that I had seen. So I inherited an organization that was now insolvent, but had one of the best strategic plans on paper in the state. Talk about a disconnect!

We re-built our organization from that rather inauspicious start, but the memory never left me. Mission statements, and all the strategies in the world are not going to make any difference, if in fact you do not have a clear method to get the plans off the paper and into action. "We fulfill our mission"—a statement that is a great example of why an organization succeeds, and conversely why others fail. As a leader of an organization, what strategies can you follow to insure that you can implement your plans?

Nuts and Bolts Strategies:

- You must undertake a true strategic planning process. Once you have that plan in place it must be fluid. It must be revisited and revised in a timely manner. We urge you, as a Director or CEO, to arrange with an outside individual or company to help you organize a process and write a strategic plan. This plan should have goals and objectives, and benchmarks to prove to you, your key donors, and your clients that you have achieved the goals you have set forth.

- Develop an operational plan that uses your strategic plan as its base. You should also develop action plans by departments, or areas. This would include priorities, timelines, person responsible, budgetary impact/cost and a completion checklist. There must be measurable benchmarks and outcomes to demonstrate to yourselves and to external audiences that your organization makes a real difference and has real accomplishments.

- Implement a strong evaluation component. The term evaluation is threatening to many. But, in this case, we are evaluating our progress to our plan. Develop milestones and evaluation checklists to insure that you are making every effort to meet the mission statement. I do not view evaluations as a negative to staff. Rather, it is a method to help them become more effective in their job. I cannot emphasize enough that good leadership does not use evaluations as a threat, but rather as a tool to help employees and organizations succeed. Consider both formative and summative evaluations. That is, consider periodically reviewing where matters stand and what you and perhaps other key leaders can do to help a program, an office, or perhaps even an overworked individual achieve the task at hand. Then there should also be annual, summative evaluation—what did we set out to do, did we do it, and at what cost?

"No one has a monopoly on virtue"

Why was this statement so important? I thought long and hard about its implications to my organization, leadership of organizations, and the relationship between the organization and our community. I think, over time, I grew to understand how to use this statement to better serve our mission:

Nuts and Bolts Strategies:

• Don't "fall in love" with your organization to the point where you can no longer see your position in the overall scope of things. As a leader, one must believe deeply in his or her organization and its mission—but, as this statement says, it is not the only mission in the community or world that has value. Understanding this reality allows the organization and leader to collaborate, and build the organization within the overall needs of the community.

• Be willing to respond to the needs of other organizations/ circumstances within the community. Two examples come to mind:

In 1993, our part of the country had the worst flood in a century. People in the community lost their water supply for several days, and others lost their homes. Our organization did not have a mission in this area. However, we used some of our volunteer base to help in a number of the efforts during this difficult time. The good will we earned came back ten-fold compared to the "lost time" off of the job. And, our volunteers felt good about helping our community in a time of great need!

As with many organizations, we conducted an Annual Campaign. We intended to begin this campaign organizationally in August, and to made actual donor calls beginning in September through December. A number of our "donors" were heavily involved in the annual United Way drive. They asked if we would be willing to delay the start of our campaign a couple of months. Our organization was not a beneficiary of United Way funds, so it would have been easy to have ignored the request. However, we did delay our Campaign, and did so for a number of years so as to not conflict. Once again, our organization benefited from the "good will" that our action received from the community.

- Develop that shared community value within your organization. Volunteers are the heart of any non-profit organization. For long-term growth and stability, it is critical for organizations to continually develop strategies to build their volunteer base. Not every potential volunteer will have the same interest level and commitment as that of the organization's leaders. By understanding the "monopoly of virtue" concept, an organization can develop strategies to broaden the horizons in the areas of volunteer recruitment.

Summary:

This chapter outlines critical initial internal organizational points. During difficult times, a non-profit organization must "center itself". It must develop a clear and focused mission. It must develop shared priorities. The organization must develop a clear and measurable strategic direction. This strategic direction must "get off the paper" through operational plans that include a strong evaluation component. As the organization moves through each of the above steps, it must not lose sight of its overall role in the community. It must develop a philosophy of shared community values and interests. If properly implemented, the organization is now ready to move to the next step.

"Tough Times Require Tough People"

In the best of times, operating a non-profit organization can be difficult. The organization is a business, yet often the business is "cause related". So often we hear the message "you can't run this like a business". Experience has taught that there is a fine balance between running a non-profit organization as a business, without sacrificing the "heart" of it. This is especially true during tough economic times, with increasing competition for scarce financial resources. How does one compete, how does one sustain the organization without losing its "soul"? These are questions asked throughout the years, throughout the world of non-profit organizations.

In tough times, it is critical for the leader to step forward. This manual is not about leadership principles but that is where it starts. Everyone is looking to the Director and Board for leadership and will follow it—either direction. The following are critical to organizational success:

Nuts and Bolts Strategies:

- The Operational Executive must accept the leadership responsibility for the organization. It is not something that can be pushed to the Board. It is a requirement for the position.

- You will notice that we said *responsibility, not role*. There is a critical difference. The operational head accepts the leadership responsibility for the organization, but it may in fact not be the individual that takes on the public role. The following example will shed light on the difference:

> There was a chapter of a non-profit organization that was in deep financial difficulty. The state in which the non-profit operated was in tough economic times, and revenue coming into the non-profit was dropping, and as a consequence services were being cut. Needless to say, morale was at an all-time low, as people saw jobs eliminated, and unmet needs increased. The Director of this Chapter was a "program person". She was one of the best in the country at delivering services to clients, and the technical aspects of running the chapter. In fact she was nationally recognized for these abilities and achievements. Unfortunately the territory had changed, and those skills were not as important as revenue generation, public speaking, marketing, and "schmoozing" potential major donors. The Board faced a dilemma—members could fire her and hire someone who had the required new skills, or develop other strategies. The Director understood the dilemma and also clearly understood her responsibilities. With outside volunteer help, she developed a strong marketing plan, targeted public relations efforts and went to the Board with her plan. She was not a public speaker, but her love of the clients that the chapter served was obvious to all. Her strategy was to use others to do the initial public speaking, and as part of their program, she would just tell a couple of stories about the clients to various

organizations and groups. She never "made the ask"—
she left that to others. The strategy worked! The
organization fought through the tough times. The morale
of the organization was raised; the Director did not fall
away from her leadership responsibilities, and frankly
saved her job.

- As a leader, it is critical to understand both your strengths
and weaknesses. It is also very important to build a strong
network of volunteers and outside help to fill in the gaps of
the organizations administrative abilities. Vanity and ego are
not good skills during tough times. A good leader, who wants
to survive the tough times, surrounds himself or herself with
the very best talent that is available.

- The leader must see through the eyes of the followers.
Experience has shown that those who lead, but don't have
the ability to relate to those that "follow", ultimately
underachieve or fail. True leadership includes team building,
shared visions, and ultimately power sharing. Those that build
an organization that they can "control" often are the first to
fall during the tough times. A true example:

The organization had a Director who, over a
period of years, put his own people on the Board. It was
a gradual process, but over time, the Board became "his"
Board. Virtually every Board member that was nominated
over a several year period reflected the Director's views
of the organization and mirrored his strategic direction.
All went well for a number of years. Board meetings lasted
less than a couple of hours, there was no real committee
work, it was all staff driven, and during the good economic
times, the organization was stable. There was little
program development, no participation growth to speak
of, and over a period of time the chapter fell far behind

the rest of the non-profit world. It was not computerized, because the Director was not computer literate. The staff did not have the computers necessary to grow the organization, there was little staff development—in summary the organization was ripe for failure. At first the fall came slowly; donors and service groups fell away, and staff left. Eventually the inevitable happened—an economic downturn. The Director and the Board were in trouble—past due bills, a declining and disgruntled volunteer base, and client complaints. The end result was not good. A local reporter was alerted to the problems and this resulted in publishing an ugly newspaper series. The Director was fired, the Board disbanded and eventually reorganized. It took a number of years to rebuild the chapter.

This is a true case study of misguided leadership that caused a solid non-profit organization to fail. It was a style of leadership that made no effort to see through the eyes of the followers, and ultimately fell apart.

- An organization's ability to survive difficult times ultimately falls on the leadership and its ability to sustain the morale of the organization during the difficult times. This is a well-understood precept but there is more to it. The question is how to position the organization before the tough times to insure that morale will sustain itself during the difficult times. Some additional strategies that have worked through the years:

  1. It is critical to develop a solid communication system for the organization. The organization should communicate not only the success of the program, but also the cost of this success. This should be done in the good times as well as more difficult times. Newsletters should include donors,

volunteers, as well as other key identified market segments. It is important to make sure that people understand the budget, the use of funds, and the breakdown of expenses. They must understand the financial picture of the organization prior to any economic downturn. This will insure their trust when funds become tight.

2. Contributions, financial and in-kind, are often a result of relationship building. It is so important during good economic times that the organization's leaders build relationships with donors. As economic conditions tighten, those organizations that have forged the strongest bonds will be the ones whose contributions are more easily sustained. It is very important that donors receive communication from the organization outside of the normal financial appeals. Many successful organizations develop quarterly donor communications. It is also critical to develop Board or leadership representation with key donor constituencies. If a Foundation, civic organization, or business is a major donor, efforts should be made to gain their representation on committees or the Board.

•   Volunteer morale is critical to the success of the organization. Volunteers and donors thrive in positive appeals and reactions, not negatives. Paint a positive picture—if the picture is bleak, be realistic but not without painting a picture for the future. Strike a vision for the future, and demonstrate the organization's ability to follow a disciplined path to attain that vision. The volunteers will respond to a leader who recognizes the problem, and shows the toughness and discipline to overcome it. After all, if the challenge is external [difficult economic times], then many non-profit organizations are facing the same challenge and so your honesty, enthusiasm, and clear vision will help your organization succeed.

• Employee and staff morale have a tremendous impact on an organization. Staff members often have more interaction with volunteers and clients than the Board or Director. As circumstances become tough, it is essential for staff members to view the Director as involved and committed to the issues faced by the staff. As funds decrease, and programs face cutbacks, the Director must become more involved with the staff. The Director must share the organization's challenges. Thus, the Director must keep the staff completely informed as to the financial circumstances of the organization. Decisions should be made as a team rather than in isolation. This will insure a team approach to the over all community and Board. So, schedule and hold regular staff meetings. Keep and widely distribute minutes of those meetings. Include the financial status of the organization in the meetings.

• Board morale is often overlooked. I cannot tell you how many times that I have heard Directors or Board members complain about a lack of commitment or interest by other Board members. While this is a problem at all non-profits, many successful ones follow some form of these strategies:

1. Develop a Board limitation component to the Board policies and procedures. This prevents someone from staying too long and dominating an organization. It also promotes a good Board rotation that includes turnover and continuity. So, if you have a nine member Board of Directors, have them serve, for example, three year terms, and each year, the terms of three members expire—or perhaps six year terms,

and every two years, the terms of three members expire. This allows both for continuity and for fresh ideas and new blood on the Board.

2. Develops strong committee structures. This insures that the Board members become active and involved. Give the committees real tasks, and realistic time lines to achieve those tasks.

3. Develop a method to allow longtime Board members to stay active in the organization after they leave the Board. This is usually in the form of an Honorary Board of Directors. It is important that the organization make efforts to keep these members informed of all issues.

4. And, frankly, require Board members to attend meetings [at least three of the four quarterly meetings a year], annual retreats, and at least some of the events or programs that the organization sponsors. They need to be visibly involved, and this involvement will encourage workers and other supporters.

It is critical that the organizational staff understand that Board members are still volunteers. As volunteers they often have many pressures related to their own careers. It is critical to the Board's morale that you keep members informed, and their time is not wasted.

Summary:

Organizational morale and leadership are absolutely critical to the survival chances of a non-profit organization during tough economic times. The Director and Board must work closely together to develop strong communications efforts to donors and volunteers. Systems should be developed to insure information and programs get communicated outside of the normal financial appeal channels.

Leadership is vital to the overall success of the organization. The Director must develop strategies that target staff, Board, and the overall volunteer sectors. The central mission of the organization must be the focal point, and the Director must communicate a strong vision for the future. You cannot and should not hide problems; rather you need to present them in their true form to the organization. The leader must have the mental toughness to inspire the Board, staff, and general population. This comes about when the Director is viewed as understanding the issues, committed to attacking the problems, and has effectively communicated a vision for the future.

"A House is only as strong as its Foundation"

Tough economic conditions can bring even the very best non-profit organization to its knees. For those organizations built on a foundation of sand, their future is bleak at best. As conditions deteriorate, an organization faces really two choices; make changes, or face the prospect of failure. It is at this crucial time that an organization cannot make mistakes.

A common mistake that is often made during tough economic times is to focus all energy on "hunting the cash". While attracting additional resources is critical, it will not alone solve the problem. Instead, the successful organization should follow a three-pronged strategy:

1. "Expand the Infrastructure of the organization"
2. "Fine tune the message and delivery system"
3. "Hunt the cash"

Expand the Infrastructure of the Organization

Tough economic conditions stretch an organization in many different negative ways. Morale, leadership, commitment, and focus are all tested. For many, unfortunately, it is the culmination of a deteriorating infrastructure that probably started long before the economic downturn. The Board may have become lazy, or dominated by the agenda of one or two long time members. Or the good and committed Board members may have left, and their replacements were not of the same level. There are endless ways things can silently deteriorate for an organization. An example:

I met with the Board of a non-profit organization that was in trouble. How did this organization arrive at this point? Well, for many years the organization was successful. It had a solid Executive Director, and an equally good Board President. Two Board members raised the funds. They made all of the calls, and delivered the cash. Unfortunately, one of these two Board members retired, and the other gradually "burned out". There was no real committee structure in place, no real organization to the process, and contributions declined. The make-up of the Board was flawed. Most members were "program" people with no real business or development experience. When the economic downturn hit—the organization was in trouble. The Executive Director moved on to another position with another organization and the organization was now faced with a Board with no executive leadership, and no expertise in the area of raising dollars. Morale had sunk to the absolute pits. The organization had few resources to attract a top new executive, and the financial drain was increasing. As I met with the Board, obviously the members' first inclination was to "hunt the cash".

They had already made mistakes by approaching donors with poor presentations or appeals, and had "fouled the nest". A quick but solid recovery plan was needed if the organization was to survive—a plan that was both comprehensive and supported by the organization. It was at this time that a three pronged strategy was initiated and over the next year it was touch and go for the organization. Fortunately, it was ultimately successful.

Nuts and Bolts-Expanding the Infrastructure of the Organization:

The following outline specific strategies that may be chosen to follow in expanding/strengthening the foundation of the organization:

- Conduct a detailed Board Survey. That is, you should distribute this survey to each Board member. It should include:
    1. The member's concept of the central mission of the organization.
    2. Organizational priorities.
    3. An assessment of the individual member's expectations and experiences to date as a Board member.
    4. An evaluation of the organization by the Board member.
    5. Suggestions by the Board member as to what changes s/he would like to see take place.
    6. Provide the Board member with an opportunity to volunteer in an area of expertise.
    7. Ask the Board member for suggestions as to other individuals s/he feel would be an asset to the Board or organization.

- Provide a summary of the survey to all Board members, though consider how much you wish to protect the "anonymity" of any given Board member to encourage the most honest answers.

- Use this summary as a "kick-off" point to the annual Board Retreat. If the organization does not have one, it should begin that process.

- Develop a Board mentor program. This will insure that new Board members are properly prepared for their responsibilities as Board members.

- Develop a firm Committee structure to the Board. Each committee should have a chair and a co-chair. This means each committee has a written agenda and also keeps minutes, which it submits, to the Director for each meeting. Committees should be encouraged to meet quarterly, and on as "as need" basis. Each committee should have a *Committee Cookbook*. The "cookbook" should include:
    1. Past minutes and past timelines for committee.
    2. A description of the responsibilities of the Committee.
    3. A description of the responsibilities of a Committee member.
    4. A timeline for the committee.
    5. The committee's evaluation of progress for the previous year.

- Rotate committee membership and leadership. Ideally committee memberships would be for a two-year period.

- Each committee should be asked to give a report at the quarterly Board meetings.

- The Board President and Executive should retain copies of all committee reports and actions.

- Committees should present the Board with action items as needed.

- Consider forming an Honorary Board of Directors. The Honorary Board is critical to the expansion of the infrastructure. It provides:
    1. A means to keep good past Board members involved with the organization after they leave the Board.
    2. A means to "move" inactive Board members without alienating them.
    3. And there may be people in your community who are willing to lend their good names—but only their good names—to assist your organization; their good and well-known names might open doors that otherwise would be closed to you. So consider either an Honorary or Advisory Board, something that allows you to enlist such help and only requires at most coming to an annual dinner to be thanked.

- The Board and Nominating Committee should determine a list of Board membership targets/requirements. These may include:
    1. Major financial contributors or representatives. This is especially true for major corporate support.
    2. Civic and service organizations that are critical to the success of the Board.
    3. Specific professional expertise—this may include medical, insurance, legal, and finance.
    4. Experience has taught that the more diverse the Board, the stronger the community support base.
    5. Different levels of income. Do not just become a "big money" Board. There is a need and a place for

"program" people, and lower income volunteers.
They too will broaden the base of the organization.

- The Executive of the organization should make every effort to contact each Board member once per quarter outside of the normal Board meeting structure. This process will insure the "relationship building" that is critical to both the short and long-term success of the organization. It is important to communicate with Board members in good times as well as bad. And, as the Director, consider calling each Board member right before a meeting but after the advanced agenda has been distributed. Don't face any unwelcome surprises at the meeting; ask if there are questions or concerns—and answer them truthfully and be prepared to respond at the meeting. The idea is to avoid surprises where possible for you and your Board.

- Careful thought should go into the structure of Board meetings. Allow time for Board members to interact with each other. There is nothing more debilitating to an organization's foundation than to have people at Board meetings that do not even know each other. If there is time, consider a social function for the meeting. That is, if some members of your board come in from out of town, perhaps begin with a dinner the previous evening to allow for socializing and informal team building, and then start the meeting early and promptly the next morning. If your members all live in the community, perhaps begin with a private breakfast at 7:30 am for example and then at 9:00 am begin the board meeting in another room at your location.

- Every effort should be made to **"connect"** Board members to the organizational services, clients, and program. The closer the bonds the stronger the commitment, and the more vibrant the organization.

- The organization's staff should become active with the Board. Staff reports should be included at Board meetings. Staff recognition by the Board should become an annual event. Board members may be able to facilitate staff-development opportunities.

- Develop an annual Board Recognition event.

- Develop an annual Donor recognition system.

Nuts and Bolts-Expanding the Board:

Almost every non-profit organization agrees with the value of building a strong Board. However, not every organization is attractive to prospective Board members, nor does every organization have the recruiting ability to expand the Board. The following are proven strategies that organizations may follow in building their Board.

- Current and past Board members can be excellent resources in Board recruitment. The Executive should develop a referral system for them.

- Local colleges and universities provide excellent opportunities to recruit Board members. Most educational institutions encourage employee community involvement. Many non-profits at all levels have used this outlet to recruit new Board members. And such people can bring real and valuable expertise, and, if faculty become involved, perhaps they can bring along eager students as volunteers.

- Local civic and service groups are excellent resources for Board members. Many members are very committed to their community, and are looking for a non-profit organization to "adopt".

- Church groups and youth groups leadership are also excellent resources.

- Many corporations' encourage/reward employees for civic involvement. They are an excellent resource for prospective Board members.

- Breakfast and Lunch business groups have been an excellent resource for organizations. Many are recruited just by an Executive or organizational member speaking engagement.

Summary:

A non-profit organization is only as strong as its infrastructure. The Board of Directors must be focused and involved. The above section has outlined specific strategies that can make a positive difference. It does not take a great deal of revenue, but it does take time, effort and organization. During tough economic times, the non-profit organization must rely on its core of support. It is obvious that an organization will not survive unless the support base is active, knowledgeable and committed. It is critical that all organizations make the commitment to not just chase the dollars, but build a strong stable infrastructure.

"Marketing 101—

Sharpening the Message"

Under normal conditions, a non-profit organization faces many difficult challenges. It is a very competitive environment to attract financial resources, quality staff, and volunteers. However, when the economic times worsen, and the financial picture for the organization darkens, these challenges are magnified. Tough times will bring out not only the weakness in an organization, but also can provide the organization with significant opportunities. One of the most important is the opportunity to "sharpen the message".

Earlier in this manual, we spoke of the importance of a unified mission statement and priorities. Now it is time to expand the mission statement and priorities to an action plan that is taken to the overall community. It is now time to re-visit the overall marketing plan of the organization. The following are nuts and bolts suggestions:

Nuts and Bolts—Marketing 101:

- The organization needs to write a Marketing Plan. We understand that you may already have one; even so you should revisit it. The Marketing Plan must include three critical areas—clients/service, development resources, volunteer/ support people. As you review the following, we emphasize that you should develop plans for each of the areas. For example, you will have a market analysis for the fundraising that is different than your marketing efforts to expand participation or increase your client base. The following is a format that has proven successful:

1. A Market Analysis:
   a. Characteristics of the industry.
   b. Trends in the industry.
   c. Major applications of your organization's service.
   d. Who are or will be your major "customers".

2. Target Markets
   a. What are the major market segments that you will penetrate?
       1] What barriers do you face in each segment?
       2] What strategies will you use to "attack" each market segment?
       3] Prioritize each market segment.
       4] What are the costs of each segment in regards to time and resources?
   b. Timelines and action plans and evaluation.

3. An analysis of your competition:
   a. Who are your challengers?
   b. What is your strategy to compete with them?
   c. How does your service compare in the eyes of the general community?
   d. What is your specific strategy to gain a competitive edge on your competition?

4. Reaction from specific "customers".
   a. What prospective customers have you talked with?

    b.   What was their reaction?

    c.   Are they willing to provide your organization with a positive reference?

5. Marketing Activities:
    a.   Marketing strategy.
    b.   Organization's promotional plans.
    c.   Geographic penetration—what are your priorities?
    d.   Segmentation, application, and marketing activities priorities.

6. Sales Activities:
    a.   How will you identify prospective clients, donors, and volunteers?
    b.   How will you decide whom to contact and in what order?
    c.   What level of "sales effort" will you have?

The section on marketing and marketing analysis is of critical importance. The organization must develop market segmentation strategies, and a true operational plan to meet those strategies.

• Evaluate the current effectiveness of your organization and message. Develop "focus" groups and ask them key marketing questions. Often an advertising agency will donate or reduce costs to help Non-Profit organizations. This information is vital in planning and honing the organizational message.

• Set a series of Brainstorming sessions. Bring in people outside the organization and ask them for input in regards to marketing, and public relations. An example:

A non-profit organization was in trouble. The volunteer base was dwindling, the Board was stagnant, and revenue was decreasing. To combat these issues, we established a marketing club. We recruited a dozen marketing/PR professionals from the broader business community. We asked them to come for two meetings, each two hours in length. Each meeting was a "brainstorming" session. We wrote every idea on paper taped on a wall. After the first meeting, we had over fifty new ideas to promote our organization. We used the second meeting to refine our list; we grouped and prioritized the ideas or projects. Those two sessions were critical to the turnaround in our organization. Over the next year, we increased revenue over $250,000 above budget, and increased our volunteer base by over 30%! The ideas served as our marketing and promotional foundation for two years. It was one of the best ideas that we ever developed.

- Reach out to the community. As marketers of your non-profit organization you can never have enough information. Survey your clients, your donors, your volunteers as to:

  1. Their perception of the organization.
  2. Their evaluation of the communication of the organization.
  3. Their evaluation of their experience with the organization.
  4. Suggestions that they may have to improve the organization.

Experience has shown that those organizations that reach out to their constituencies for feedback usually improve. Those that refuse or try to control that feedback are less effective in good times, and suffer during the bad.

- Contract with a "clipping" service. This will provide the organization with a detailed breakdown of the publicity that is generated for the organization. It will provide the organization with much data as to what is occurring, what generates publicity and contacts for future activities. Or, perhaps, use the world wide web to search the literature if you have time and perhaps a volunteer who is particularly computer literate.

- Recruit a marketing professional to the Board of Directors. This individual is critical to both the short and long term good of the organization. Often, advertising agencies in your area will provide names of interested employees to a non-profit organization. Local colleges and universities are also very good sources for marketing students, or faculty members. Perhaps an interested faculty may make your organization the subject of a practicum course for a semester.

- Develop a marketing committee to the Board of Directors. This committee would consist of Board members, and would help the organization implement the Marketing Plan.

- Develop an organizational "speakers" bureau. This would be composed of key members of the organization that would serve as speakers to service, civic, or breakfast clubs in the community.

- Develop a short video program that speakers for the organization can use. The video can be used to target the specific message that is the greatest need of the organization.

- Carefully review all printed material that the organization distributes.

- Review all communication systems within the organization. This includes response times for information requests, return phone calls, or other types of communication.

- Review the web-site status of the organization. More and more people are obtaining information from web sites. This should be a strong consideration for the organization.

- Take the time to carefully position the organization. This takes both time and input.

A great example:

> The first year I was the Director of our organization, I had a speaking engagement at a Rotary luncheon. I had the game plan down. I had a seven-minute video about our organization that I would show—it was very emotional, and then I would close with some inspiring comments. My plan then was to have a respected member of their organization in the back, with a plate to collect checks as they left our program. Well, all went according to plan. The luncheon attracted more than 80 attendees. The video was perfect—when it was over there was not a dry eye in the house. I gave a magnificent close, and as the people left the room, they thanked me as they dabbed their eyes. Unfortunately, when I went to the plate we had collected a grand total of $75.00! I was shocked. Needless to say, that was the last time we used that format or video. We went back, and re-did our video presentation. We put music to it, and we made sure there was a lot of uplift to the message. The rest is history. When I took it out the next time, there was not a tear in the place. Instead, there were a lot of smiles. Contributions went through the roof! We used that video and approach for almost two years, and the results were incredible. I learned

a critical lesson. People may feel sorry for you, but if you want to motivate people to donate or volunteer, the message must be upbeat and positive. I have shared that message with all of the non-profit organizations that I have counseled over the years, and I have yet to have one come back to me and say that my message was wrong.

Summary:

It is no accident that some non-profit organizations are more successful than others. Many non-profits chase dollars, **without** doing the key marketing and planning efforts essential for success. An "ask" without a good message is ineffective. An organization **must** take the time to develop a solid marketing strategy. Organizations that are successful reach out to the community for input. They survey their organization, as well as involve marketing professionals in the process. They develop a Marketing Plan, and prioritize their efforts. They develop a strong community component, in the form of speaker's bureaus. The organization must sharpen its message. The ability to simply and consistently communicate the central focus and mission of the organization is critical to success. An organization must properly position itself in the marketplace. Once properly positioned, the organization will not only survive the tough times, but also be prepared to successfully "hunt the cash".

"The Heart of the

Organization"

The "Heart" of most non-profit organizations is the volunteer. Regardless of the relative strengths of the mission, Board, and staff, a non-profit organization will have difficulty without a strong and committed volunteer base. In visiting many non-profit organizations through the years, we have found one key trait again and again—those that had a strong volunteer base survived, and those that did not floundered. During difficult economic times, the volunteer becomes even more critical to the organization. They provide services that the organization could never financially support, as well as serve as a base for expanding the development effort. It is essential for the organization to expand and utilize them.

Nuts and Bolts: Expanding the Volunteer Base

The three "R's" for volunteer management are (1) Recruitment, (2) Recognition, (3) Retention. Each is critical for the non-profit and we will discuss them serially:

Recruitment:

- Develop a volunteer recruitment planning system. This

must be as formal as the organization's budget, marketing, or development plan. It should include:

1. Number of needed volunteers per activity.
2. Time frame needed.
3. Special volunteer requirements.
4. Organizational Recruitment Strategies.
5. Recruitment responsibilities.
6. Cost.

- Implement the volunteer needs into the overall marketing plan of the organization.

- Set an annual goal of expanding the volunteer base by a minimum 10% per year.

- Develop a volunteer tracking system. This will enable the organization to expand its database. For example, if Joe Smith has volunteered for the Fall Walkathon, a good system would insure that he would be notified prior to the event next year. Proper tracking will insure that no one is overlooked who may have volunteered previously.

- Establish an ad-hoc committee to review the volunteer recruitment process. This committee would have a short "window" and offer its report to both the staff and Board.

- Develop an **"Each one-Reach one"** program. In this program, your organization encourages each volunteer to bring at least one new volunteer to the organization. Awards can be given to the volunteer that brings in the most new people to the organization.

- Develop a "user friendly" method to distribute volunteer recruitment material. This may include day of the event, web site, flyers, and phone registrations.

- Develop relationships with local corporations, service groups, civic organizations, schools, labor unions, and/ or small business groups. These are excellent resources for volunteers. A number of non-profit organizations have had great success in assigning venues, or specific tasks to a specific group.

- Develop special events where the general public can attend. At these special events, provide each participant with volunteer information.

- Provide volunteer sign-up information with Development efforts. Donations historically increase when a volunteer component is included in the experience.

Recognition:

Volunteer recognition is critical to the vitality of the organization. When done properly, volunteer recognition can serve as a cornerstone for the organization. People like to know that their time and effort mattered and was appreciated.

Some strategies to consider:

- Develop a formal volunteer recognition program. Successful organizations have used either Board members or ad-hoc committees to develop this program. Often it is an "end of the year" culminating event. You should formalize criteria for awards.

- The organization should insure that every volunteer receives a thank-you. It may seem small, but non-profit organizations lose thousands of volunteers over the course of the year, by simply not thanking them for their efforts.

- Many organizations develop special Volunteer Awards. They are made to the top volunteers.

- Publicize past winners of volunteer awards. This builds a sense of tradition in the organization. Consider a release to the media after the annual volunteer recognition, with photographs, and brief biographies. Let your volunteers and the larger community know that you value those people who donate their time as well as their financial resources.

Retention:

Many organizations focus on volunteer recruitment but neglect the critical aspect of retention. They lose as many "out the back door" as they bring in through their outreach efforts. A good non-profit organization:

- Carefully tracks their volunteers.

- Develops a database that insures that each volunteer is registered.

- Develops a system that enables the organization to communicate with each volunteer at least twice per year.

- Develops a system that facilitates feedback from volunteers.

- Designs a volunteer recruitment effort that is "user friendly" for the various age groups that may help the organization.

- Carefully evaluates volunteer retention on a year-to-year, or event-to-event basis.

- Targets the responsibility of volunteer retention to one individual or committee.

Summary:

A Non-Profit organization is only as good as its volunteer commitment. The non-profit "graveyard" is full of organizations that fell in love with their mission, but disregarded the importance of the volunteer. During difficult economic times volunteers gain in importance. They can:

- Take over tasks for which the organization had paid employees or external consultants in the past.
- Provide needed manpower for an expansion of revenue producing events.
- Provide new creative ideas for the organization.
- Become a source for additional revenue.

During tough economic times, many organizations turn all of their energies to financial matters. That is a mistake that must not be made. Volunteers are the heart and future of any non-profit organization. The good ones understand it, and focus on it during the tough times.

"Counting the Beans"

No one can dispute the importance of finance and the budgetary process for the non-profit organization. Regardless of program quality, or the virtue of the mission statement, a non-profit organization must be financially sound. While this manual will not focus on accounting systems and process, we believe it important that we discuss strategies that are critical for success.

Nuts and Bolts—Strategies for "Counting the Beans" effectively:

The following are strategies that many non-profit organizations have used successfully to gain/maintain a sound financial foundation:

- There should be a Budget/Finance Committee of the Board. This committee should meet quarterly and provide the Board with updated financial statements. The Budget and Finance Committee should consist of individuals who have a sound understanding of accounting principles and finance. Accountants, bankers, CFO's are all good sources for committee members. In the event that a Board does not have this expertise, it should retain outside advisers until they are able to recruit a Board member with this background.

- The Budget and Finance committee should work with the staff to develop an accounting system that not only reports the financial status of the organization, but also enables the staff to use the reports in conducting their daily operations. It is important for department heads to have access to their budget numbers **and** more importantly where they are in regards to expenditures vs. budgeted numbers.

- It is critical that you develop a firm budget calendar. It is important to develop a calendar so that all departments of the organization have input into the process. You need to insist that departments submit budgets, that there be adequate discussion and consultation, and that these departments receive approval of their budgets before the fiscal year begins. "Ownership" of budget numbers is important for a non-profit organization—the good organizations involve staff on the front end of the process, not just the back end. Consider back-up plans in case revenue falls below projections [where would you cut back?] and also in case revenue greatly exceeds projections [are there any other first class projects you should be doing?].

- Many good non-profit organizations carefully develop the revenue side of the budget at the same time as the expense side. The organizations that have financial problems are those that base their budget solely on projected expenses, without taking into consideration developing a true revenue side. An example:

> A non-profit organization was in trouble. "We can never keep a Development person long enough to become effective", the Board members lamented. It was true that over the last two years the organization had hired and lost four Development Directors. The Board had not conducted any exit interviews, so the reasons for the turnover were unclear at best. However, during a consulting visit, a red flag emerged—the organization's

budgeting process. It seems that one Board member historically had developed the budget for the organization. He interviewed each staff member as to the department's financial need, and came to a final determination of required expenditures. I asked him about the organization's revenue side projections.

"We must raise whatever final number that we determine the expenses to be," he said. He went on to say that over the past two years there had been an increasing significant revenue shortfall. He also admitted that the Development turnover in large part was a result of frustration and inability to attain the fundraising goals.

I asked the reason for not involving realistic historic revenue projections as part of the budgetary process. No answer was given. Needless to say, the Board changed its procedure to include revenue projections as part of the budget process. At last look, the current Development person had lasted over a year under the new system.

- The Board/staff should develop an Emergency financial plan for tough economic times. It is absolutely critical to become pro-active rather than reactive during difficult times. Let me be more specific:

  1. Each department has a budget. As part of the process, each department head has identified certain expenditures or activities that can be postponed during tough financial periods. Thus when the organization sees the tough times coming, it can reduce expenditures in a controlled and planned manner.
  2. The Director, or Board, identifies key milestones for the budget that, if unmet, immediately warns the

organization of pending financial difficulty. Once identified, the organization automatically moves into its emergency budgetary status. Expenses are reduced—be it travel, supplies, new purchases etc. This safety valve enables the organization to overcome short-term difficulties.

3. The organization should have a financial plan goal of having a minimum of twelve months expenditures in reserve. This looks good on paper, but in reality experience has shown that having nine months is a realistic goal for many non-profit organizations. The reserves must be liquid in nature.

4. The Board should approve the Emergency Financial plan guidelines. This will insure that the organization does not have internal difficulties during tough times.

- You should share financial data with staff and throughout the organization. While obviously salaries are kept confidential—it is important to keep everyone properly informed of the financial status of the organization. Everyone in the organization should take "ownership" of its financial condition.

- The Board should provide ongoing staff development in the area of finance. Often non-profit staff members have excellent training in program areas, but little finance background. Workshops, seminars, or continuing education should be considered.

- The organization should have written investment policies that guide the Board.

- The organization must retain professional investment advice if the Board does not have that expertise.

- Finally, and we assume this is already done, you should have so-called D&O [directors and officers] liability insurance. You will find it easier to attract important business people in the community to your board if you can assure them that they will not suffer potential personal financial loss if the organization is sued and loses. D&O policies are relatively inexpensive, and, in the sense of attracting a first-rate group of key volunteers, it is essential.

Summary:

A good non-profit organization has a solid budgetary process. The process includes revenue projections as part of the final budget determination. The Board is actively involved, and a Budget/Finance committee is responsible for the process. The budget process is inclusive, with staff members having input to the final budget determination. The organization should develop an emergency budget plan, and set milestones in place that will alert the organization to increasing financial problems. The Board should provide the staff with ongoing finance/budget training. This training could be in the form of workshops and seminars. The budgetary process is a critical factor for organizational success. It is important that the Board develop a simple solid budgeting system.

"Getting it off the paper and into action"

One of the greatest skills in an individual and organization is the ability to "get plans off of paper" and implement them. This is not easy. Often organizations get heavily involved in the planning process, but neglect the implementation stage. Staff members become overworked, resources become scarce, the reasons vary, but invariably organizations in trouble usually also have trouble getting plans off paper and into action.

In meeting with troubled non-profit organizations through the years, several common faults have recurred again and again:

- Often Strategic Plans do not reflect the operational capabilities of the organization. The Strategic planning process is incomplete, and does not take into consideration the staffing responsibilities and skills.

- The organization does not truly understand its strategic strengths and weaknesses. It develops plans that do not reflect its true strengths.

- The organization develops a plan but does not include the individuals that are needed to implement the plan into the process.

- There are no formal operational considerations associated with the strategic plan.

- There are no evaluation systems associated with the plan.

- The organization does not share timelines and priorities.

- The strategic planning process is flawed, and non-inclusive.

Nuts and Bolts Strategies to "Get it off the Paper":

The following are specific steps that can help an organization become more action oriented.

- Undertake a time utilization study for the staff. The organization must be able to answer the questions "what do you do, how do you spend your time?" This will help the staff and organization in the planning process. It will prevent the mistake of asking an overworked staff member or department to undertake additional responsibilities. And, frankly, as many corporations reposition their resources, including personnel, your organization will do better in approaching these corporations if you can demonstrate you have reviewed tasks and resource allocation and made appropriate, yet difficult decisions.

- Undertake a strategic internal and external analysis of the organization. This should be done by an outside source. This will help the organization better use existing limited resources, identify opportunities, and develop realistic plans.

- Develop a skills list for the organization. This would include staff, Board, and key volunteers. On this list, specific individual skills would be identified. This list offers significant help in the planning process. It does no good to develop a new initiative, when the organization has neither the requisite on-site skills, nor the resources to retain those skills from outside the organization.

- The organization should develop a consistent format for planning. An example would include:

Task Resources Person Res. Projected Cost Timeline X Off-

- Operational plans should be shared with the staff. This will insure good communication, and unity. Staff members will understand the time constraints and responsibilities of co-workers.

- The Director will delegate operational details to those that are going to be asked to implement those plans. In an ideal organization, the staff will be a part of a team that collaboratively plans for the organization. Without a sense of "ownership" for the staff, it will be difficult to get the "buy in" necessary for operational success.

- The organization develops a team oriented non-threatening environment. This is critical to bring out the best in an employee. S/he must feel free to "extend" herself or himself at the risk of failure, and s/he must not fear evaluations. Evaluations should be viewed as a necessity to help the organization move forward, as a means of individual and organization improvement, rather than a means to reward or punish. Many organizations undertake "team building" seminars with outside consultants.

- The organization must focus on communication. Priorities and resource allocations must be communicated throughout the organization so that there is no internal bickering. There is a standard athletic maxim that can be applied to all non-profit organizations—"Before you can win, you must learn not to beat yourself". Good communication will insure that a non-profit organization does not "beat itself". Many non-profit organizations develop annual retreats for staff and board. This procedure can facilitate team building, and also improve communication.

- An organization must undergo a strategic planning process. A trained individual should facilitate it. The organization must ultimately be responsible for the design and implementation of the plan. It is also critical for the organization to involve all key stakeholders in the planning process.

- As part of the hiring process, the interview should include operational questions. For example "Explain your process for implementing . . ." The organizational culture must reflect a balance between operation "nuts and bolts", and the theoretical.

Summary:

An organization is only as good as its ability to put plans into action. It is not a difficult process to develop a strategic plan. The difficulty lies in the implementation of that plan and, frankly, linking the plan with real budgeting, financial decisions. As a non-profit organization, there are many stakeholders with different interests, priorities and commitment levels. An organization cannot survive and prosper without a means to organize those divergent views into a single cohesive plan. The ability to get it off the paper is a key operational and leadership skill. It requires detailed operational plans, evaluation systems, and most of all a commitment by leadership to "walk the walk, not just talk the talk".

"There is no limit to what one can achieve if no one cares who gets the Credit"

This is an athletic maxim that is an essential building block for a good non-profit organization. The line that many coaches over the years have said to athletes is that there is no "I" in "Team." We can trace countless examples of underachievement to a lack of a cohesive team approach to an organization. Think about it, how many times have you seen well thought out solid strategies **not** accepted because of jealousy or lack of unified support?

Examples abound:

> I was called to visit a non-profit organization. The Board felt that there were problems, for Board members had received staff complaints and wanted an "outside" appraisal of the situation. As I sat down with the Executive Director the problem quickly became clearer—there were significant management style issues. While in his office, staff members constantly interrupted us. They were coming to him for his blessing or approval

for virtually every action step in the organization. I asked him if that was a normal occurrence, and he said "No, today is actually a little calmer than normal because you are here." I asked if I could meet with staff members individually. He approved, only if he too could sit in on the meetings.

Well it did not take long to establish that the Director was a "control" person. He needed to micro-manage the entire organization. Staff members walked softly around him, and would take on no initiative without first obtaining his approval. It was an organization devoid of creativity, energy, and ownership. I was able to sit in on several staff meetings. The only person who spoke was the Director. If a staff member had a difference of opinion or new idea, it was obvious that s/he had to carefully position it so that the Director felt it came from himself. It was sad. At the end of the visit I asked the Director his opinion of his staff—"Great" he said. "It was tough early until I was able to get my team on board, but now we really work well together." I asked him his opinion of the cohesiveness of the staff and the communication process. Once again "great" was his answer. I asked if he felt that the organization was moving at the speed and direction he wanted—"no question". I asked if the staff felt the same way "sure!" His management style and ego had totally isolated him from the true reality of the organization.

The Board was very disappointed with the direction and momentum generated by the organization. The Board and staff had real concerns regarding communication, energy, and management style. If something were not done quickly, there would be real problems. The end result was not good. Over the next several months, staff problems escalated; and over time the Board became divided. The Director could not change, and within a year the Board asked for his resignation.

As a consultant, it was a very frustrating assignment. The problem was obvious, but the leader refused to even acknowledge or modify his management style. It would not have taken a great deal of change on his part, because his staff was very committed to the mission of the organization, and the Board was solid. But he would not change; therefore problems festered, and the situation dramatically worsened. The organization became fractured, and there was no semblance of unity or team. The only recourse was to change leadership—and they reluctantly made that decision. Unfortunately it took the organization over a year to recover from the change. It was not an easy time, and the clients of the organization suffered.

Another example:

The Executive Director of a Chapter was in trouble. She had a divided staff. There was infighting, and sometimes staff members would go days without speaking to each other. The environment was horrible—one could "cut the air with a knife". What happened? For many years the organization had consisted of a few staff members in somewhat small physical space. It had struggled to exist, and the staff had grown very close to each other. But fortunately for the organization, it started to grow. With the new success came expansion. The organization hired new staff, implemented new initiatives, gained additional revenues; and suddenly the small little chapter had gone to the next level. Unfortunately the new staff and the older staff never really "connected". In the past the organization worked as a team and there were no conflicts or rivalries for resources nor were their "egos" involved.

It was a team approach all the way. With the growth came the problems, and the organization started to wilt under the pressure. It got nasty. The Executive Director was caught totally unprepared as jealousy, pettiness, and back-stabbing ran rampant in her organization. Eventually the problems exploded out of the office and into the Board. Older staff members went to longtime Board members with their concerns, and the new staff members went to the "new blood" that had come in with the "revival". The Executive Director was caught in the middle and told by both sides to "solve the problems". It was a long and tough task. It sapped her energy, as well as the momentum of the organization. In fact, to this day, the organization has not been able to regain its momentum. On a graph, it had peaked, flattened out, and gradually declined.

The infighting was ugly and very difficult to end. Eventually the organization had to ask for several talented staff members to resign. Several Board members also resigned during the process, contributions declined, and the image of the organization was tarnished. Frankly it could have been much worse had the Director not stepped in and taken concrete steps to end the problems.

Nuts and Bolts—Strategies to build a Team:

Many of the following are obvious, but often ignored. They are proven strategies used by the successful organizations.

- Communication is a critical component for a team. The organization must develop a system that promotes good communication. Some ideas:
    1. The Director needs to schedule and hold weekly staff meetings. Consider distributing agendas prior to the

meeting. Consider also allowing staff members to have input in regards to the agenda. Keep summary minutes, distribute and use them as a resource for future meetings.

2. Departmental meetings should have a regular schedule. You need to ensure that agendas and minutes are distributed and filed with the Director.

3. The Executive Director must take it upon him/herself to initiate ongoing communication with staff members. There must be an open door policy where staff members feel comfortable talking. The Director must be seen as "engaged" in the process.

4. The Director and staff together should develop a "covenant". This should include:

   a. Methods of handling disputes, or communication issues.

   b. Promises not to bring outside problems into the workplace.

   c. Methods to solve grievances.

5. Set one time aside per month as an informal group activity. If nothing else, have pot luck luncheons, and be sure to bring a "home-made" dish. Encourage trading of recipes. One non-profit established a "tie" exchange. Everyone who worked in the organization would bring in a necktie, typically a particularly ugly tie, and everyone would have to take away a tie. The result was lots of laughter, and an easing of the typical workplace tension.

- The organization must have a set Grievance Policy as part of By-Laws of the organization.

- The Board should have a Personnel Committee that includes someone with a strong Human Resources background. The Committee should present for Board approval Personnel Policies and Procedures. They should then be distributed to the organization. No one should be allowed to go outside the outlined procedures. This includes Director, Board and staff. Grievance procedures should be outlined, and followed.

- A strong evaluation system should be implemented. The Executive Director should conduct a formal evaluation of each staff member. This should be conducted on an annual basis unless otherwise required. The Board, through the Personnel Committee, should conduct an annual formal review of the Executive Director. Some very good organizations include self-evaluation as an important tool for staff members. They should include the employees view of their:
  1. Strengths.
  2. Weaknesses.
  3. Areas to improve.
  4. Methods they are going to utilize to improve.
  5. Needs from the organization to better do their job.
  6. Top priorities.
  7. Organizational concerns.

This has proven to be very effective in improving communication and production.

- The Board and staff should have an Annual Retreat.

- Specific Team-Building activities should be planned for the staff and director. This is very effective if conducted by an "outside" entity.

- The Board of the Directors must be committed to a strong functioning Committee structure. This structure will insure communication and interaction with the organization's staff. I have yet to see any organization that has a strong Board Committee structure have major personnel issues.

- The Executive Director should make every effort to attend at least one leadership seminar or training session per year. A Director is never too experienced to learn new methods or ideas.

- A culture must be developed in which each person is encouraged to bring out the best in their co-workers. Team-building workshops can be very helpful in this area.

An example:

I visited a non-profit chapter out of our region. In speaking with the Executive Director, it became obvious that there was an increasing problem that she was facing with two staff members. It seemed that one of the members would come to work at 7:30 am and work until 4:00 pm on a daily basis. He became upset because one co-worker in a different department would come at the normal 8:00 am hour, and would often be seen talking to other staff members, with the general appearance of not being in his office. Often this second co-worker would leave the office early. The conflict was growing.

In speaking with the Executive Director, there was not a work issue. The two employees just had different work "styles". One worked steadily throughout the day, while the other worked in "spurts". Both were highly effective in their respective styles for the organization, but a clash seemed inevitable. The Executive Director handled it beautifully. She held a team-building workshop. At the workshop, the facilitator brought out the different types of work styles and asked each to describe their most effective style. That process started the communication process. The staff members started to respect each other's style, and the two individuals actually became much closer.

The Executive Director did a very good job of eliminating a problem in her staff. She started by first understanding the different work styles of each of her staff. She respected both, and rather than stifle either staff member, she devised a strategy that was non-threatening in which they could better understand each other. It is no accident that she has one of the top non-profit organizations in her state.

Summary:

The summary to this chapter is very simple—"Before you can win, you must teach your team not to beat itself". The top organizations are not ego driven. There is excellent communication, unity of purpose, and shared priorities. The Board has an active committee structure, with firm Policies and Procedures. Each area understands its role and is committed to the overall mission of the organization. Team building workshops are a part of the organization's annual plan. The key leaders undertake ongoing leadership and team building training. In conclusion, the organization understands "there is no limit to what one can achieve if no one cares who gets the credit."

"The end of the Beginning"

We are now at the ending point of Section One of the manual. We wrote this section to offer the non-profit organization and executive some concrete "Nuts and Bolts" strategies that if implemented can properly position the organization to survive during difficult times, and flourish during the good ones. It is assumed that the organization has carefully reviewed the basic principles previously outlined. Now you are in a stronger position to begin the process of "getting the dollars".

The next section will focus on developing a solid revenue plan and strategies to attract additional revenue. The writers of this manual have been in positions responsible for generating over fifty million dollars. Hopefully some ideas will be help, as we address:

Developing a Revenue Plan
The Annual Campaign
Special Events
Grant Writing

SECTION II.

Nuts and Bolts—
"Getting the Dollars!"

Developing the Revenue Plan

In a previous section, we discussed the need for an organization to include a revenue plan as part of the budgeting process. This is very important to an organization because it will enable the organization to develop a "true budget".

The revenue plan should include projections for the organization to generate revenue. It will include projections from the following areas:

- Corporate Contributions
- Grants
- Annual Campaign (Giving)
- Special Events
- Deferred Gifts
- Individual unsolicited gifts
- Miscellaneous
- In Kind Gifts

Assumptions:

- Corporate gifts: This category includes business contributions. These gifts usually come from the Charitable Giving of the company.

- Grants: This category includes Individual, Governmental, and Corporate Foundation Grant gifts.

- Annual Campaign: Most organizations have an Annual Campaign program. This usually comes as a result of an Annual Appeal, usually run in the 4th quarter of the fiscal year.

- Special Events: This category includes special events operated by the organization to generate money. It may include Golf Tournaments, Auctions, Walkathons, etc.

- Deferred Gifts: This category is very difficult to forecast. It may include a variety of gifts including cash, property, or stock.

- Individual unsolicited gifts: Every organization should have an annual historical record of unsolicited gifts received from individuals.

- The organization may generate income from a variety of other methods including rent, license fees, or other organizational activities.

- In Kind Gifts: The organization should benefit from in-kind gifts. They may include goods, or services donated by individuals or corporations.

- Projected new contributions in each area.

Nut and Bolts Strategies for Developing the Revenue Plan:

- In the Revenue plan, good organizations use historical data as a baseline for future projections. For example we would itemize those corporations that had a 3-year history of giving to our organization:

Projected Revenue—Corporate

Company	3yr. Ave. Gift	Prop. Ask	Date	Caller	Contact
XYZ Co.	$4,500	$5,000	Jan.	Ligouri	Davis
B Inc.	$10,000	$12,000	Mar.	Dobbs	Jones

• The organization must develop a strong Development Data Base for each Corporate Gift. It should include if possible:
  1. Company name.
  2. Giving History.
  3. Key areas of interest.
  4. Contact—any important information regarding the individual or corporation.
  5. Date to contact.
  6. Assigned Caller.
  7. Additional notes on each corporation as needed.

• The organization must individualize the contribution request. It should be based upon a history of giving (or lack thereof) as well as the areas of interest of the corporation. The organization must do its homework *prior* to the request. An example may offer insight:

> A non-profit organization ordered a Chamber of Commerce list. The Executive Director had no real development experience. He decided to write a general letter, addressed "To whom it may concern" with a generic ask for a $1,000 contribution to his organization. He enclosed an organizational brochure with a return envelope. Everyday he rushed to the mail waiting for the revenue to flow into the organization—nothing happened. His mistakes were obvious; he failed to do any homework on the donors, had not identified a specific need for the gift, and expected to generate funds with no relationship to the donor. Unfortunately, he also lost

potential donors who may have given to the organization had he done a better job of doing the homework and building a relationship.

- It is critical for the Chief Executive Officer of the organization to develop a high profile in the community. Contributions are usually much higher if a relationship exists with the organization. Many corporate and individual donors prefer to have a relationship with the top person in the organization. Seldom will a CEO give significant dollars to someone under the CEO's level. An example:

> The Executive Director of a Chapter did not enjoy interactions with the private sector. He was very comfortable in his special area of expertise, but was very uncomfortable with anything outside his comfort zone. Instead he expected the Board and Development area to raise the funds. This cost the Chapter significant dollars, and more importantly, it lost a competitive position in the community. Revenue for the organization was never consistent because the level of expertise and commitment of the Board varied. The Development area positioned the organization with donors, but there was no "closer". The organization slowly lost market share, and as a result, services were reduced.

The Executive Director should consider membership in:
1. Breakfast and Luncheon Clubs.
2. Civic and Service organizations.
3. Corporate and College Boards.
4. Other Charitable organizations.

- The organization/Board should provide the Development staff and the Executive Director with ongoing training in sales/marketing. This may include attendance at sales seminars, or meeting with a company's sales management staff.

Summary:

Before an organization can develop a realistic budget it must develop an Annual Revenue Plan. This plan will serve as the basis for projecting income. The Revenue plan will be the cornerstone for the final operational plan in the Development area.

It is very important for an organization to develop a sound tracking system for donors. This will enable the organization to target the appeal to a specific interested individual or area of interest for the company/foundation. This requires a great deal of homework. It is the responsibility of the Development area of the organization to organize the tracking system, and properly position the organization with targeted donors. In many instances volunteers are involved in the Development process. The organization (Development area) must provide the volunteers with the proper data, prior to the call. It is important for the Chief Executive Officer of the organization to become actively involved in the development process. The higher the community profile, the easier the development task. The organization's staff must develop the revenue plan with the Board. This will enable the Board to assume a level of ownership in the plan as well as help in accessing key potential donors.

The Annual Campaign

Virtually every organization has some form of annual appeal or campaign. This is usually set for a set time period, with set development goals. This manual will not go into detail in regards to the Annual Campaign appeals, but instead will focus on Nuts and Bolts Strategies that have been successful.

Nuts and Bolts Strategies for Annual Giving:

- While the Annual Campaign/Drive is usually for a set time period, it must be understood that this is a year-around project. A timeline for the annual campaign may look like this:

    October-December Annual Campaign.
    January-March—Clean-up follow-on activities— (recognition event).
    April—Evaluation of the Campaign—What worked, what did not?
    May-June Design meetings for the next Campaign.
    July-August Database research, volunteer recruitment, supplies and materials.
    September—Volunteer training, and organization.
    October-December Annual Campaign.

- The Annual campaign consists of both in-person and direct mail appeals. The following is an organizational chart:
  Development Office.
  Development Committee of the Board.
  Team Captains (# and segments are determined by the organization).
  Teams (formed by team Captain).

- The Annual Campaign design:
  1. Development Office and Board meet to design the campaign.
  2. The Development and Board determine the number of teams that are needed for the campaign. They may developed special segments to include Medical, Legal, and other identifiable interest groups. Ideally someone in the market segment will chair it. This group will develop the overall contact list to the campaign, as well as targeted asking amounts.
  3. The Development and Board recruit Captains. The Captains are responsible for a team of volunteers that will make calls on targeted individuals and businesses.
  4. The Development office will train the Captain on their responsibilities.
     a. The purpose of the campaign.
     b. The operational details—donor cards, etc.
     c. The size of the team.
     d. Team member's responsibilities.
  5. The Captain will recruit team members.
     a. The team will be responsible for reviewing the contact list.
     b. Team members will sign up for individuals or businesses.
     c. They have the option for making additions to the list.

6. The Development/Board will review each team's sign-up contact sheets.
   a. In the event of duplication, they will determine the contact assignment.
   b. They will contact each captain with the unassigned prospects.
7. The Development and Board will host a meeting for all campaign teams.
   a. Review the purpose of the Campaign.
   b. Motivate the volunteers as to the importance of the Campaign.
   c. Review the Campaign organization.
   d. Review the Campaign's operational design.
   e. Review the final campaign contact lists.
   f. Set the next meeting.
8. Most organizations set bi-weekly captain's meetings during the campaign. The meeting is held to insure that the campaign is moving forward.
9. The Development Office will provide all campaign volunteers with ongoing progress reports.
10. There will be a close out Captain's meeting.
11. A Campaign recognition activity will occur.
12. The organization will develop a method to obtain feedback from the volunteers.

- Most good Annual Campaigns identify key major donors prior to the start of the campaign. The Board or President usually takes responsibility for making the call on those major donors.

- All directions to the captains and team members should be in writing. This insures consistency within the campaign.

- The Board and Staff are responsible for prospects that are not selected by the teams.

- Any Direct mail appeal is followed by a phone call.

- Printed material for the campaign includes informational brochures, presentation folders for major donor appeals, campaign pledge cards (may be attached to the brochure), and Business Reply Envelopes.

- All campaign pledge cards are returned to a centralized location.

- Every donor receives an individually addressed thank you letter.

- Every donor is entered into the database.

- Each Board Member is expected to contribute to the Annual Campaign.

This is a basic outline that has proven successful for many non-profit organizations. However, some non-profit organizations do not have the resources to support a Development office. These non-profits must become more innovative in their approach. They may:

- Contract with a professional consulting firm to organize and conduct their annual appeal. Some of these firms will work on a contingency basis. Their fee is based upon the amount of revenue that they produce. While this enables the organization to control costs, it can cause problems. The organization must insure that the outside fundraising entity properly "respects" the organization's name and reputation. A number of organizations have retained the wrong firms and have had negative public relations problems.

- Develop a strong Board commitment to the Annual Campaign. In this case, the Board basically undertakes the campaign as its responsibility

- The most effective and safe method is:
  1. Bring in an outside consultant
     a. Organize and design the campaign.
     b. Help in the volunteer recruitment.
     c. Organize the infrastructure.
     d. Make targeted Calls.
  2. Train the Board to conduct a majority of the campaign.

Summary:

The Annual Campaign or Drive is an excellent proven method to raise significant funds for an organization. Its organization is difficult in the first year, but over time it becomes easier and larger. Many organizations increase revenue on an annual basis. During tough economic times, it is critical for an organization to have a "grass roots" development effort. There is no substitute for personal relationships in effective fundraising. The Annual Campaign provides the organization with a proven method to expand individual contacts. For those organizations that do not have the resources for a Development office/individual, there are options. The most effective is a combination of professional consultant and Board commitment.

Special Events

Special events are an excellent method for an organization to raise both needed funds, and positive public relations. Too often organizations view special events as solely fund raising events. That is a mistake! Some events may indeed be major fund raising efforts; Annual Golf Tournaments, Walkathons, and Bicycle rides are examples. However, non-profit organizations use Special Events in several other key ways:

* To increase volunteer involvement.
* To develop relationships with other organizations or businesses.
* To reward clients, staff, volunteers.

Nuts and Bolts Special Events:

Increase Volunteer Involvement:

As previously stated, an organization is only as good as its volunteer base. In many instances non-profit organizations have used simple special events as a method to build their volunteer data base and recruitment effort. For example:

> A number of years ago, our Chapter wanted to establish a cycling program for the mentally disabled. Often this required special equipment, or volunteer requirements. As part of our "kick-off" we hosted a bicycle-riding event.

We held it downtown, on a weekend; we obtained sponsors from a local radio station, bicycle shops and civic groups. We hosted a lunch in a downtown plaza after the ride for all participants. All participants also received a T-shirt. Some of our mentally disabled athletes also rode in the event, and many came to the picnic. We lost money the first year, but it was a great success. From that event, we:

1. Obtained a civic group that sponsored our state competition.
2. Found a radio station that adopted us as their Charity for the next year.
3. Received numerous equipment donations.
4. Recruited volunteers to coach our "special" athletes.
5. Expanded sport expertise to help our program staff.

This was a great event for us. It had an incredible positive long-term impact for us. We did not do it to generate money, but over the years it grew to become a very positive revenue event.

• Develop relationships with other businesses or organizations: This develops a sense of shared community values and awareness. An example:

Several years ago, our Special Olympics Chapter wanted to raise our identity as an athletic organization as compared to a social agency. At the same time, an organization was promoting a touring golf tournament that featured retired Major League Baseball players. The tournament would be a one-day event, with a silent auction held the evening prior to the event. Revenue was to be shared between our organization and the Retired Baseball Players organization. We held the event, and we did not make money from it. But the overall results for the organization were tremendous.

> We had TV coverage of the event, with our athletes alongside former Baseball stars. Numerous community members played in the tournament because they wanted to meet the baseball stars, but gained a tremendous awareness of our athletes. At the post event banquet, our athletes were shoulder to shoulder with several Hall of Fame members! What a thrill for our athletes! The benefits from this non-revenue producing event were huge for our Chapter.

The Baseball-Golf tournament did not raise significant dollars for our organization. However it was a great event for our community, and raised our profile as an athletic organization. The benefits far outweighed any negatives!

• Reward Clients, staff, and volunteers: Special events can provide an excellent reward to staff, clients and volunteers. An example:

> Several years ago, as part of our State Chapter Summer Games, we decided to host a concert. We contracted with the "Up with People" organization. At the time, this group was very popular. Many thought that we would host the concert and sell tickets. Many thought it would be a great fundraiser. Instead, we decided to host a "free" concert. All of our athletes, coaches, families, and volunteers received "tickets" in the mail. We distributed others to civic groups throughout our host community. This event cost our organization several thousand dollars—however, it also gave us a tremendous opportunity to recognize, thank and expand our relationship with the community. Needless to say the response was incredibly positive. Interesting enough, we also received a number of unsolicited contributions to help us defray the concert's cost.

This is a concrete example of "how" an organization can use a special event to thank and recognize key groups. It was a great success. The community has successfully hosted that event now for over fifteen years. The organization and community are now inseparably tied together.

- The organization should make every effort to involve radio stations in planning and implementation of special events. Many radio stations will co-op the advertising for a non-profit organization.

- The organization should meet regularly with ad agency personnel. Often ad agencies will "adopt" a non-profit organization. They can provide ideas, as well as talent.

- A Special events calendar should be developed. Many good organizations try to have some type of public event quarterly.

- Special events that are to raise significant dollars are dependent upon obtaining sponsorships and in kind gifts. These enable the organization to reduce costs for the participants, and heighten the margin of profit.

Nuts and Bolts: Organizing a Special Event

Organizing a Special Event is absolutely critical to the insuring the event's success. The following are critical components of Special Event organization.

- Over the years, we have found that the most successful special events are organized into a strong committee structure. This insures not only a year one success, but also continuity to the event. Each committee:

1. Should have a Chair and a Vice-Chair. This protects the event and the organization in the event of a sudden departure of the Chair. It also provides a "training method" for new leadership.
2. Each committee should also have a secretary. The secretary should keep minutes, and collect a copy of all of the activities of the committee for the event. For example, the committee secretary will keep a record of where the supplies were purchased, the cost of the supplies, and the reliability of each supplier. The secretary should also develop a timeline for the event that can be used for future events.

- An Event Steering Committee should be formed. The Steering Committee is composed of Chair of each Committee, as well as staff or other volunteer members.
The Steering Committee should elect a Chair, Vice-Chair, and Secretary.
    1. The Chair is responsible for the overall organization of the event and oversees the committee activities.
    2. The Secretary is responsible for coordinating the material developed by each committee secretary. They will eventually be responsible for the developing a "cookbook" for the event that can be used in future planning efforts.

- The following are several committees that have been effective. Obviously they may vary dependent upon the Event. Over the years, experience has shown that good non-profit organizations and special events have many of these committees in place.
    1. Public Relations—Responsible for promoting the event, recruiting volunteers and participants.
    2. Logistics—the Nuts and Bolts of the Event itself. This may be divided into several sub-committees.

3. Fundraising—May include ticket sales and other areas of raising funds for the event.
4. In-Kind gifts—Identifying areas for In-Kind gifts for the event. This lowers the overhead, and raises the "profit" level.
5. Recognition—Thank you to donors, *volunteers*, and participants.

• At the end of the event, the organization must conduct a thorough evaluation of the event. Each committee should be asked to participate. Each committee should provide the steering committee with their views on both their specific area as well as the event. This should be conducted within two weeks of the event.

• From the evaluation, the steering committee and organization should develop a list of action steps to improve the event for the following year. The action plan is really a series of steps the organization and steering committee plan to take to improve the event for the following year.

• The "Cookbook" for the event should be filed at the Non-Profit organization.

• The organization should use the cookbook as an organizational tool for staff efforts.

• Many successful non-profit organizations develop relationships with media outlets (radio, TV). The outlets promote the event and participate in some way with it. Often the media outlet promotes the event on an in-kind basis. They are seldom willing to donate cash to the event.

Summary:

The Special Events component of the revenue plan is critical during tough economic times. It enables the organization to reach out to new potential donors and volunteers. If organized properly, special events also raise public awareness of the organization. Special events can provide many positives to the organization far beyond revenue. The organization must take a long-term strategic view of special events. Many mistakes are made by non-profit organizations in this area. Too often they focus on the revenue benefit alone, instead of the other positive outcomes of the event. The top organizations use special events during the difficult times to raise morale, awareness, as well as revenue.

It is very important for the non-profit to carefully develop an organizational format that is consistent with the organization's strengths. Volunteers are critical and you must carefully recruit and nurture them. Many organizations have staff that will also participate on the Steering Committees of the event. However, some non-profit organizations are so limited as to staff, that this is not feasible. Those organizations must expand their recruiting efforts to get committed volunteers to take over those responsibilities.

Special events can make the difference for success or failure for a non-profit organization. They can be used to expand the geographic impact of the organization, as well as to gain additional resources and revenue. They can also keep the organization's name in front of the public during difficult economic times. They also serve to rejuvenate existing volunteers, staff and clients. During the down times, organizations must be creative, color outside the box, and keep pushing ahead! That is what separates the winners from the losers.

In-Kind Gifts

In kind gifts are often the most overlooked source of "revenue" for an organization. Many organizations have not reached their potential in this area. We define in-kind gifts as those presented to an organization that are in goods/services rather than money.

Nuts and Bolts Strategies for Increasing In-Kind Gifts:

- As part of the Budget process, an organization should identify costs. This will provide a basis for making qualified in kind appeals. For example many organizations have major copying and paper expenses. These expenses are usually fairly consistent. By identifying the costs, the organization can then go to companies, or suppliers and ask for some or all as an in kind donation. Organizations throughout the country have received accounting services, copy paper, copiers, envelopes, printing, office supplies, cell phones, etc.

- Once the organization has identified potential in-kind needs, publish it to your organization. Many call it a "wish list". Regardless, make your needs known; often an individual cannot contribute money, but can help in many other ways.

- Publicize the in kind gifts that you do receive. Publishing an in kind gift is a great positive for an organization. It demonstrates to others another way they can help.

- Survey similar organizations in other geographic locations. Often they develop relationships that your chapter can "steal" and present. Sharing in kind sources and special events ideas is an excellent way to expand an organization.

- Develop a Board and key volunteer lists that identifies their areas of expertise and business. They are often your first source of in kind gifts. It is important to research your key donors, and target the request. Do not expect to receive, if you never make "the-ask".

- Include an in-kind gift needs list for every special event or activity for the organization. Remember, for every dollar you save, it is one less that the organization must raise.

- Cultivate in-kind donors as you would a prospective cash donor. Too many organizations do not ask for in-kind gifts.

Summary:

In kind gifts can make the difference between success and failure for a non-profit organization. The organization must identify needs, present "the-ask", and recognize the gifts. In kind gift often reach a different type and level of donor. Do not underestimate the value of it.

Up to now, we have discussed critical factors that must be in place for a non—profit organization. We have established a revenue plan, and discussed the Annual Campaign as well in-kind gifts. It is now time to take a detailed study of grant writing—an often misunderstood and underutilized tool for the non-profit organization.

SECTION II:

Nuts and Bolts:
Grant Writing—
"Getting the Dollars"

I. Introduction

There are a series of activities that together comprise the development of a proposal for external funding. These activities fall into three broad categories: pre-proposal research and writing, the writing of the proposal for submission, and the post-proposal activity.

A. *Pre-proposal phase*

1. *Assessing/Evaluating Your Program—strengths, weaknesses, opportunities, and threats [SWOTS!]*
2. *Defining the Project*
3. *Putting an Idea into a Project Format*
4. *Identifying Potential Sponsors*
   a. Foundations
   b. Corporations
   c. *U.S. Government*
   d. Other
5. *Ascertaining Sponsor Interest*

B. *Preparing a Full Proposal*

1. *The Narrative*
2. *Project Evaluation*
3. *The Project Budget*
4. *Key Personnel*

II. The Pre-Proposal Phase

A. *Introduction*

Long before you actually write a grant proposal to a specific funding source, there are many necessary steps that you need to take and, if undertaken properly, will help increase the percentage of funded proposals and thus improve one's grantsmanship. If this part of the process is not undertaken or is undertaken improperly or less than completely, the grantseeker may obtain funding for a proposal that cannot succeed or s/he will approach inappropriate funding sources or a flawed proposal will fail to gain funding from a prime funding source. TOO OFTEN, GRANTSEEKERS DO NOT ENGAGE IN A SERIOUS PRE-PROPOSAL REVIEW; DON'T BE GUILTY OF HASTE.

There are three key steps in this pre-proposal phase:

1. Evaluating one's own program honestly and accurately;
2. Undertaking a needs assessment of the population the program serves or the problem the program attacks; and
3. Researching the world of funding sources to find appropriate sources to which to apply.

B. Strategic Planning

If the Bard suggested that "to thine own self be true," it certainly is true in the grantsmanship process. There are several points to consider, and you should have come to certain conclusions from reading Section I of this book. Still, a review can be useful, and here it is:

1. What is the current size and scope of the operation you are representing [which may be as large as the entire institution or as small as a particular program or office]?
2. What is the current role and mission of this operation? [In a sentence or two. If you cannot summarize succinctly and clearly, perhaps your organization is somewhat fuzzy on its mission and objectives.]
3. What are the strengths and weaknesses of the operation? [Don't overestimate strengths and don't underestimate weaknesses!]
4. Does the operation work? that is, does the organization you represent make a difference in the life of the community it serves?
5. Finally, given that few grants will permit a dramatic increase in programmatic personnel, can the operation you represent realistically accept new responsibilities?
6. And what are your plans when the grant funding runs out?

In the standard language of strategic planning, one should look at SWOTS: strengths, weaknesses, opportunities, and threats. Most individuals are keenly aware of the strengths of their program and the organization within which the program fits. Few of us want to admit to weaknesses—organic, systemic, personnel, etc. Opportunities are normally the reasons you are seeking additional funds. Finally, are there "threats"—fiscal, demographic, political, social, etc.—that may affect the well being of your organization and/or program?

The grant seeker must be honest in this evaluation. Sometimes the best conclusion is that, at the present moment in this organization, grantsmanship should be set aside for a thorough review and revision. Or, perhaps, the organization is at capacity and cannot do any more very well. Or, worse, perhaps the organization is not functioning smoothly and there is no point to take on new responsibilities when it cannot discharge the existing ones very well. The point is simple, for the very worst fate for an organization can be accepting a grant and new responsibilities for which it is unprepared and/or for which it cannot meet. Similarly, a serendipitous conclusion can be that the operation is stronger, better regarded, and more capable of undertaking new responsibilities than might have been assumed prior to this review.

NUTS AND BOLTS STRATEGY: use the obligation of the annual report or annual review to ask hard questions about the operation. That is, what do you do, how well do you do it, and do you have the capacity to do more and is it in your role and mission to assume increased/added responsibilities?

Another NUTS AND BOLTS STRATEGY: regularly collect any outside evaluation and/or coverage of your organization. That is, one should set up a file folder with formal external evaluations, letters from pleased members of the community, articles in local [and, if you are so lucky, national] newspapers, etc. Also, you may wish to save articles on issues, challenges, and problems—perhaps even outcomes that are of interest to you and your organization. While it may be time consuming, these files can prove invaluable resources when you write your proposals. The Internet can be an invaluable resource in this search, and perhaps once a month you should peruse sources related to your interest area.

Now it is time to put together the necessary, brief evaluation of the program or operation you are representing as a grant writer. There should be three parts to this evaluation: history, present activities, and future plans.

1. Community based, non-profit organizations: many institutions of higher education offer course work to help train personnel for community organizations—that is, certificate programs in non-profit management. Larger organizations—the United Way, the Boys' and Girls' Clubs, etc.—probably have their own, respective, professional fundraising staff. But you may be a member of a small organization that seeks to help a neighborhood high school improve the graduation rate of its students or perhaps an organization located in a small town to assist that town's physically challenged citizens. you, too, should engage in a brief review.

HISTORY: the Glenbrook Coalition to Improve Schools was organized in 1997 to help alleviate a 30% dropout rate among 9th to 12th graders at Glenbrook High School. Over the years, Glenbrook schools have had to deal with a changing school population, including more non-native English speaking students, more single parent homes, and an increase in area youth gangs. The coalition consists of community activists, educators, and concerned business people who are seeking to devise a program to help at-risk GHS students. Students who complete the program will receive a tuition scholarship at nearby Urban State College [USC], which also cooperates with the program.

CURRENT ACTIVITIES: At first, the Glenbrook Coalition spent more time fundraising than designing, implementing, evaluating, and revising a first-rate retention improvement program. Last year, after much soul-searching, the coalition designed a literature-based retention improvement program that already has begun to improve the retention of students in the target population. External evaluations have been positive as has community support for the program.

FUTURE PLANNING: the coalition wants to raise more scholarship dollars for students who complete the program and also wants to design a summer "bridge" program with nearby USC to help graduating seniors with the transition to college.

Now, it is your turn. Set aside a forthcoming weekend to review the operation; please be honest! After completing this mostly unwritten review, write out a one or two page evaluation of the program and where it is going. If you have data that will help illuminate this brief evaluation, include it. But don't worry if you do not. Once again, share this review with at least one member of your group or organization. Seek input, and test your perceptions of your organization and its operations.

Hopefully, your review resulted in positive evaluation of the organization, its methods, operations, etc. However, if you do uncover a weakness or an area which is not as effective as you want or need, please consider bringing the matter to the attention of the organization—the director, unit head, academic dean, chairperson, etc. It would be far better to meet the challenge you have found and submit a proposal in a later funding cycle than to rush to funding with a possibly serious flaw in the operation which might imperil the success of your proposed program and the external funding you are seeking.

C. Needs Assessment/Problem Definition

There are several points to consider: defining the issue or challenge to be addressed; indicating the scope of the issue or challenge; and finally a brief indication why the organization you represent has the capability and capacity to meet the challenge successfully.

1. What is the issue or challenge? Be careful to define this in terms that lead to measurable evaluation. That is, do not define the matter as not doing well [whatever that is] and then propose to do better—how does the grantor measure effectiveness when the goal is so amorphous? You will improve retention; you will increase participation by a certain percentage; test scores will go up; welfare rolls will go down, etc.

2. What is the scope of the issue or challenge? Is the matter simply and only local? Is it local but recurs in many places within a region or across the nation? Is it a national problem for which there should be a national solution?

3. Finally, why is your organization capable of mitigating the situation or meeting the challenge? Be honest! It is quite possible that you have accurately described a real problem, but your organization, as you analyzed it, is not capable of meeting the challenge. In many ways, you are setting goals and objectives that are within the capacity of your organization to realize and that are measurable and demonstrable. You may also wish to consider why your organization can meet the challenge better than other organizations.

The authors have sat on too many grant panels and foundation review groups and read proposals, very earnestly written, that take a great deal of time to recount a problem which is national in scope and perhaps of great depth and challenge and never, ever make clear how and why it affects the service area of the grant submitter, how the submitting organization has the capacity to help meet the challenge, and why it is the appropriate organization or vehicle. Grant readers are very practical people; they have only so many dollars to award, lots of worthy agencies and/or organizations seeking funding, and they want real measurable outcomes so that they can, in turn, demonstrate that the resources they make available make a real difference. The more you help them realize their goals, the more likely you are to receive funding. So don't pass over this step lightly.

Now it is your turn. Take out some paper, and consider: what is the issue or challenge? What is the scope of the issue or challenge? Does your organization have the capacity to meet the challenge? How?

D. Plan of Action, Project Design, or Methodology

Having defined the challenge or need you wish to address and having defined it in a series of concrete, measurable goals or objectives to realize, you now have to think about a plan of action. That is, you need to put together the specific steps the organization would have to take to achieve the goals and/or meet the objectives you have set forth. This section in your planning must be very specific: what specific activities, what specific methodology [for a research proposal], or what target populations? You may even wish to include a timeline, since that will help demonstrate just how specific your plan of action and its accompanying activities will be.

In very brief format, you may also wish to outline briefly other key parts of the final written proposal to help match your proposed course of action with external funding sources. Thus, you may want to compile some preliminary budget figures, suggest some of the key personnel involved in the project, and also outline a simple but effective evaluation plan.

For non-profit organizations: the Northwest Church Coalition for medical services to seniors wants to test a pilot program to help bring needy seniors the medical services they need and deserve. Working with the nursing program at Downtown State University, churches in the area will bring diagnostic medical services to seniors who regularly attend eight area churches. The pilot program will seek to convince health insurers and medical care providers to bring such services to the churches.

The two-year pilot program will commence with a workshop to train nursing students at DSU to deal with low income seniors needing medical help. A pilot program will last for 120 days. Evaluation will take 60 days, including questionnaires to the seniors, nursing students, church personnel, and medical care providers. The next 120 days will see an expansion of the program from two area to four area churches. After another evaluation, the program will expand to all eight area churches. It is believed the proving the wisdom of this approach will ensure funding after the end of the grant project.

Now it is your turn. Take a piece of paper, and write a brief summary statement.

E. Ascertaining Sponsor Interest

There are several, distinct sponsor sources. At this point in the process, you have a good sense of the organization you represent and what it can do, the new challenge you wish to meet, and the steps you believe your organization will need to take to meet this challenge. Now, you need to determine if an outside agency is interested in providing funds [and, perhaps, advice] to help you. There are four main sources of such funds: private foundations, the U.S. Government [and its many departments, agencies, institutes, and programs], private corporations, and such other sources as state and local government.

To begin, you must research the sponsor sources. Approaching inappropriate funding sources will only delay the beginning of your project. Equally important, the more you appropriately narrow your funding source list, the more likely you will receive a favorable funding decision from that source.

And, please think about partnering and partnerships.

This bears repeating—please think about partnering and partnerships. The best proposals bring together various groups in an innovative and exciting partnership that benefits the community as it is defined in the proposal. Consider how you can create win-win situations for many groups—involving perhaps a local company or chamber of commerce, perhaps a local self-help group like the Kiwanis Club or Rotary Club or Boy or Girl Scouts, perhaps a local foundation, and then a major but more distant funding source—a national company that has an office or plant in your community or a major national foundation. Partnerships work better, and frankly they are very attractive to possible funders because their support is leveraged by all the other support you obtain—a truly win-win situation! That is, each funding source can claim [a degree of] credit for the whole project while funding less than the whole.

PRIVATE FOUNDATIONS: the publications and resources of The Foundation Center are best. The Foundation Center is an independent national service organization established by foundations to provide an authoritative source of information on private philanthropic giving. In fulfilling its missions, the Center disseminates information on private giving through public service programs, publications, and a national network of library reference collections for free public use. The New York, Washington, DC, Cleveland, and San Francisco reference collections which The Foundation Center operates offer a wide variety of services and comprehensive collections of information on foundations and grants. The Cooperating Collections are libraries, community foundations, and other non-profit agencies that provide a core collection of Foundation Center publications and a variety of supplementary materials and services in subject areas useful to grantseekers. Publications, including *The Foundation Directory*, the *Source Book Profiles*, and individual *ComSearches* are invaluable in ascertaining potential foundation sponsors. Finally, the Center has a great web site, *www.fdncenter.org*, and spending some time there will be worth the investment.

There are several types of foundations:

• *Independent Foundations* are established under broad charters that mandate support of social, educational, religious, and other charitable activities. Actual giving patterns usually reflect the interests of the endowment's founder. Based on the scope of their giving, independent foundations may be further categorized as local private foundations or national foundations. From time to time, independent foundations will change funding priorities and funding limitations. Nonetheless, seek to match your project with the priorities and limitations of these funding sources.

- *Company/Corporate-Sponsored Foundations* are established and organized as entities independent of the parent company, with separate boards of directors. These foundations typically maintain close ties with the company by funding areas related to corporate activities. They also give money to organizations located near company operations and fund projects that will improve the communities where the company workers live.

- *Community Foundations* receive funds from many donors, rather than an endowment established by a single donor, and are also known as public foundations. Community foundations support projects that will meet needs of or improve the community. They often provide capital support and award scholarships and fellowships that promote access to higher education for local high school students.

- *Operating Foundations*, like independent foundations, are supported by endowment income but use their resources to conduct in-house research or provide a direct service in specific areas of interest. They make few, if any, external grants, and these usually supplement the foundation's ongoing program.

As you commence researching the world of private sponsors, you should ask "Is this project appropriate for foundation funding?" Demands for the limited resources of the private sector make it essential that foundations leverage their money to have the greatest impact. Despite the diversity of organization, several ground rules for foundation funding exist. Most foundations will only fund special projects or provide start-up support for activities that will become self-sustaining after a short period of time. They prefer to fund projects that are on the "cutting edge," representing novel approaches to identified social problems or needs. In addition, foundations seldom support projects that state and federal mechanisms can fund.

Please note that foundations do not usually provide the level of support that U.S. Government programs do. A typical grant from a local foundation runs from $10,000 to $150,000 for the length of the project; federal funding typically provides that level of support annually for several years. And, foundations almost never provide indirect cost recovery, which federal grants provide to help defray organizational costs for the grant project.

It is also worth noting that your best opportunity for foundation funding comes from the local foundations in your community. Nearly every program that seeks foundation funding has heard of the great national foundations like the Ford, Kellogg, and Exxon Foundations, but these national foundations have great demands for their great resources. A local foundation shares your concern with the quality of life in your community, and is often the best opportunity for you. That foundation may view your agency or organization as a member of a partnership dedicated to improving life where you both reside. Your problems or needs will be more real to them and more compelling. Cultivate local foundations: if you represent an educational agency, invite the professional staff to address classes on non-profit management, on community services, etc. If you represent a non-profit organization, invite them to serve on an advisory board for a project or seek their input into an ongoing activity. Involve them, cultivate them, and eventually they may become a financial supporter of your activities.

In undertaking your research, you must be realistic. Read the descriptions in the directories for all of the foundations on your list [or read their funding guidelines typically listed in annual reports made public], and ask yourself the flowing questions:

- Do the goals of the proposed project match the foundation's priorities?

- Does the foundation give to the kind of organization that you represent? [e.g., higher education, K-12, local non-profit]

- Does the foundation support projects in the geographical area for the project?

- Does the foundation support the type of project you will propose?

- Does the foundation provide the type of funding you want, e.g., seed money, endowment, construction, research, training?

- Is the foundation's grant range and period of support in line with the project's budget request?

There is a tremendous variety among foundations that reflect the varying size of foundations and of their professional staffs. Once you have determined a list of foundations, you will need to review the specific priorities, limitations, and other qualifiers of individual foundations to narrow your list. Draft a brief—no more than two-page—letter that outlines the challenge, the proposed course of action, and the qualifications of your organization and request a copy of the foundation's annual report and any other publications that will help you learn more about the foundation's funding priorities and application procedures. Check their web sites, since many foundations will provide a great deal of information on-line. For local foundations, you may suggest that you will telephone personally in two weeks to discuss matters.

Do not be surprised at this initial stage if the foundation does not invite such time-consuming steps as a full, multi-page proposal.

Here are some suggestions for approaching the various kinds of foundations:

1. Local foundations tend to network and exchange information with other local foundations. A proposal to one foundation could result in funding from several foundations—all responding to the challenge you raised.

NUTS AND BOLTS STRATEGY!

2. Try to meet the program officer or other paid staff. Various studies have concluded that as much as 80% of grants from foundations [and corporations] are done through personal contacts; make those contacts! Even if your proposal does not fit the funding priorities of a particular foundation, the advice and counsel of an experienced and highly knowledgeable program officer will prove invaluable to your grant seeking efforts.

Another NUTS AND BOLTS STRATEGY!

Ask your new friend, the local foundation program officer, to help you approach the larger, more national-in-scope foundation. These people probably meet once a year or more at appropriate conferences and workshops; use those connections—another type of partnership.

3. Write a letter of inquiry, keeping in mind the funding priorities of the independent, corporate, or community foundation. That is, do not try to fool the foundation or distort the proposal, but do try to see if there is another

way to view the proposal, a way that fits the funding priorities of the foundation in question.

4. Do not overlook operating foundations. One of the most famous operating foundations is The Johnson Foundation, which conducts operations out of the famous Frank Lloyd Wright-designed home, Wingspread, in Racine, Wisconsin. Operating foundations, if interested, can provide a site for your training operations, your conference to disseminate results, or other meetings. While these foundations cannot and will not fund a large part of your project, they can be very helpful.

5. If you find more than one appropriate foundation to approach, don't request full funding from each foundation. Foundations do tend to network; instead, consider asking them to partner with one another and with your organization. And, absolutely do not send your letter of inquiry to twenty-five or fifty or one hundred foundations like scattering so much buckshot; or, if you do engage in such an approach, do not expect much success. Narrow your list to several appropriate funding sources, and seek to meet with them, and develop a working relationship and mutual respect.

Now, it is your turn. Are foundations an appropriate source for your project? Should you concentrate on local foundations or national foundations [whether headquarters in your geographic location or elsewhere]? List several foundations, key contact people, and reasons why you believe these foundations might be interested in your project. Also, if you have an easy means of contact, other than a "cold" letter or telephone call, include that information.

THE U.S. GOVERNMENT

The government in Washington and its many Cabinet-level departments, agencies, institutes, and programs provide literally billions and billions of dollars in competitive grants each year to worthy organizations. There are many ways to learn about these funding opportunities. Among them are the *Federal Register,* the *Catalog of Federal Domestic Assistance* [CFDA], the *Commerce Business Daily*, department—and agency-Internet web sites, and various privately published compilations of federal grants information.

The *Federal Register* is the daily record of the business of the U.S. Government. No grant categories can be announced, no awards made, and no funds spent without first appearing in the Federal Register. There is a web address, *http://www.access.gpo.gov/su_docs/aces/aces140.html*, for your convenience.

The *Catalog of Federal Domestic Assistance* lists in numerical order all federal grant categories. You can obtain this information from government publications, private publications, and on-line. Again, there is a web address, *http://www.cfda.gov/default.htm*, for your convenience.

The *Commerce Business Daily* is a daily listing of federal government solicitations for research, development, and training contracts. Again, there is a web address, *http://cbdnet.access.gpo.gov/*, for your convenience.

Various privately compiled and published lists of federal grants are too numerous to review in detail. There are two basic kinds of offerings: publications and web sites that seek to abstract in timely fashion all federal grants information and those that seek to abstract in timely fashion federal grants information on a particular topic or in a particular field, e.g., business, health, or education.

There are many areas of federal funding but the most important areas [by number of programs and amounts of dollars to spend] are:
The National Institutes for Health.
The National Science Foundation.
The National Endowment for the Humanities.
The U.S. Department of Education.
The U.S. Department of Health and Human Services.
The Office of Energy Research.
The U.S. Department of Housing and Urban Development.

Once you have an idea of the federal office or program that may be interested in your proposed project, write the office to request an application and category guidelines. If you remain interested, call or write a program officer to request several successful grants from past years. Many federal agencies will make available a handful of successful grants from a past competition; some agencies will require you to file a Freedom of Information Act request—do so! Previously successful applications can provide a wealth of valuable information and guidance. Some federal agencies offer sessions to help would-be grant seekers or may entertain telephone calls or even office visits, and give you personal time at certain times of the year.

NUTS AND BOLTS STRATEGY:

Consider befriending an individual on the staff of a local Congressional representative or even U.S. Senator. Any proposal you consider submitting will be improved if it has the interest of Representative or Senator so-and-so. At my previous institution, we were fortunate to have an absolutely wonderful Congressional representative with a first-rate and very hard-working staff. We would either send our proposals through that office or we would send copies of our proposals to that office. We had a success rate higher than the average submitting organization and, while we all wanted to think that this reflected superior proposals, more interesting challenges, more innovative yet sound solutions, etc., I always wrote a very sincere thank you note to the Congress person because I truly believed that we received outside "help." Consider doing the same . . . that is, arrange ahead of time to visit with the appropriate staff person in the Washington, DC office, bring some material about your organization and its issues, and ask if you may ask for assistance. Since the elected official and the staff care about their district and the quality of life there as much as you do, the odds favor you gaining their support. Go for it!

Once again it is your turn. What federal agencies would be most interested in your proposal? Why? How will you go about approaching the agency or agencies in question? How will you learn more about what it takes to be successful with a particular federal grant competition?

THE CORPORATE WORLD: many corporations believe in being responsible corporate citizens and major players in their respective communities. Some corporations will listen to unsolicited proposals; some will announce and then seek proposals in certain fields; and finally some may respond to various kinds of public concern or pressure.

Unfortunately, there is no good single source to determine which major corporations, major operating branches of national corporations, and major plants and factories of national corporations will do in your local community. Certainly, there are profiles of corporations and their respective giving patterns. Cooperating libraries in The Foundation Center network will usually have such sources. However, you may wish to contact the public affairs office of the company or the local chamber of commerce to help determine the interests, limitations, and restrictions of the local corporate community.

Still, here are some suggestions for narrowing the list of corporations in your area. If you simply approach the largest corporations, please realize that virtually every non-profit organization, higher education institution, and school district are also approaching those very same large corporations. Try to put together a list of companies that would be interested in your proposal.

1. If your agency or institution is reasonably large, consider approaching companies with which the organization does business: the bank that handles the organization's funds, the supply and furniture company, the concessionaire.

2. read the society and community news pages of your local newspaper regularly. You may find that a major official in a local company or an official's spouse may be deeply involved in a particular cause . . . your cause!

3. Sometimes a company or a chamber of commerce may adopt a particular organization or cause as its cause for the year. Sometimes adoption means funding help; it almost always means valuable, favorable publicity.

4. Work for publicity with your local newspaper or radio station[s]. Such publicity may pique the interest of a local business or business official. Generally speaking, one or more reporters should have responsibility for the area in which you operate— e.g., education, community affairs, etc. Learn what they need and by helping them find good stories on which to report you help yourself to good publicity.

5. It may be that a local company has a public relations problem that somehow is related to your cause, interest, or proposed project. Your approach to that company may not only help your organization better serve its target population but also help the company earn community good will . . . a win-win situation!

6. You should take an opportunity to meet with the public or community affairs officer of the company. Sometimes s/he may be able to offer you in-kind services to help you approach another company, foundation, or competitive federal grants process. For example, a company may make available its printing/graphics operation, space in an internal newsletter, or other such services; many projects involve meetings and workshops, training and development. Perhaps the company will volunteer its conference space, refreshments, and supplies for such a meeting—a small cost to the company and a major benefit to you. Perhaps you might think of a few useful services to help spur the conversation. A local foundation might view your proposal with greater interest if you local corporation was providing in-kind services. Every potential grantor likes to see that another funding source is interested in your proposal.

NUTS AND BOLTS STRATEGY:

Once again, consider having a local business person assist you in your quest for funds from larger, more distant corporations. For example, a local funeral parlor owner may be past president of the national association; a local chamber of commerce director may have served on the national chamber of commerce board or a highly placed committee. These involved members of your community have connections that are worth as much as dollars— keep track of these connections [again, that wonderful clippings file from the local newspaper!], and try to involve these people in your cause.

Again, it is your turn. What companies in your local area will you approach, how, and why?

STATE AND LOCAL GOVERNMENTS: There are two main sources of funding: so-called pass through funds from the federal government and funds that originate from initiatives of the state and local governments. Your institution's government liaison officer can help you in this area, but, with the exception of such block grants, state and local governments are a distinctly secondary source of funds.

Still, block grants help fund a broad variety of community projects, especially in such key areas as drug and alcohol abuse and education, helping at-risk youth, combating youth gangs, and services to the elderly. if you believe that your organization and proposal may qualify for funding consideration in a block grant category, you may wish to call the Office of the Governor or the Office of Local Affairs [however it is titled in your state] to speak with an official to determine if state or local government is an appropriate source of funding for your project.

F. Narrowing the List of Funding Prospects

You have two goals. First, you want to compile a final list that gives you good prospects of obtaining a favorable funding decision. Second, you want to find enough possible funding sources for your idea that you either have more than one source to fund the project or funding sources for successive phases of the project.

If you have worked diligently to this point, you will have a clear understanding of your organization, its strengths and weaknesses, its opportunities, its threats, and the needs of the public it services. You also will understand the funding world, and whether there are funding sources that potentially are interested in our project.

Now you are ready to write the proposal, as soon as you write down your narrowed list of funding prospects.

III. Writing the Proposal

A. *Introduction*

There are no real tricks to writing a good, clear, and winning proposal. The grants writer needs to have a clear outline of the entire project proposal and a clear understanding of the organization and the project. The writer or the writing team [try not to have too big a team, because, as the old bromide says, "too many cooks spoil the stew"] should seek to write clearly, follow guidelines, and then ensure appropriate internal support and approval for the proposal.

Perhaps now it is time to discuss whether the organization should write its own proposal or hire a professional grants writer. It is an important consideration, and a difficult decision. There are clear benefits to having someone deeply involved in the organization and the proposed project write the proposal: interest, knowledge, commitment; the resulting proposal will be idiosyncratic. However, there are equally clear benefits to employing an external, professional grants writer: ease of writing, familiarity with the grants process, experience. One possible solution is to write the proposal oneself and look to a consultant to edit and critique the proposal. Regardless, you must face the issue, much as one has to decide whether to do one's income taxes oneself or hire a professional.

NUTS AND BOLTS STRATEGY:

While this may hurt, try reading what you are writing out loud. If you stumble as you read aloud, imagine the grant reviewer reading your proposal. Keep your focus firmly on that reviewer!

While one must follow application guidelines, generally speaking, most grant proposals will contain the following parts, however the RFP ["Request for Proposals"] titles the sections:

1. *The Narrative*
2. *Key Personnel*
3. *Project Budget*
4. *Project Evaluation*
5. *Future Funding or Next Moves [which may be combined with the section on Project Narrative, Budget, or Evaluation]*
6. *Project Dissemination*
7. *Abstract of Proposal*
8. Appendices
9. *External and Internal Letters of Support*
10. *Internal Authorization*

B. The Narrative

The major part of the proposal is the narrative. The narrative typically divides into several parts: the issue or challenge your organization wishes to address, how and why the organization will meet the challenge, why your organization is qualified to undertake the proposed project, the project management plan, and, where appropriate, how the project will continue [or not] after the funding period. This final point may mean discussion of a plan for dissemination of results.

In general, writing a grant is akin to writing a college research paper or a scholarly article for publication. There will be a grade [especially with federal grant competitions], but the funding contract and check signifies a passing grade. While the grant evaluating process may assign no points for clarity of writing, rest assured that hurriedly, poorly, and/or meanderingly written proposals fare worse than clear, clean, and appropriate length proposals. Thus, keep several points about writing in mind:

Consider also that the narrative can be used as a case statement of a sort for fundraising campaigns. That is, case statements, the heart of written material for fundraising, and the narrative, the heart of a grant proposal, share a great deal in common. If you can write one well, you can do the other, and, vice versa, if you are challenged to write a good narrative, you probably need to think about the case statements you have drafted.

NUTS AND BOLTS STRATEGY:

1. *Stick to the recommended page length*; some grant processes will not consider a proposal that exceeds the recommended page length or even recommended page format. There are many grant submitters who can tell sad tales of proposals returned, failing "technical review," for being longer than the allowable page limit. Equally important, an overly long proposal can numb an evaluation panel which, given the vast number of proposals it must judge, may read your proposal superficially rather than closely. While we will discuss this point later, try to put yourself in the place of the reviewer when writing, and keep within the recommended page limit.

I have been on review panels where the reviewers stopped reading at the end of the recommended page length, so if the grant indicated a narrative of 35 pages, for example, the reviewers stopped at page 35, and then downgraded the proposal for failing to answer some of the required questions. Don't play games with formatting [e.g., Times New Roman 8 to shrink a rambling narrative into the appropriate page constraints or Courier 14 because, frankly, you don't have much to say].

NUTS AND BOLTS STRATEGY:

2. Apportion the proposal properly; do not spend too much time describing the problem [which may be very well known or not particularly original] or the need to meet its challenge. Instead, divide the proposal so that each section receives an appropriate amount of attention— no section is too long and, more important, no section receives superficial or inadequate attention.

    In terms of general advice, organize the narrative to meet the evaluation criteria for the proposal. Federal grant RFPs, for example, will list the evaluation points and criteria; foundations typically have brief descriptions on what topics to cover in the proposal. Use one or more of these models for a corporate proposal. Again, view the proposal as reviewers will and you are more likely to receive that favorable funding decision.

    I have been on many federal grant panels, and the federal agency staffer will note the evaluation points and criteria and tell the reviewers, like me, to award points based strictly on these guidelines. So, for example, if one passes over the section on "Key Personnel," one may lose 5 points out of 100 points in a highly competitive process. Or, if one misapportions pages so that there is little space for the evaluation section or the plan of management section, again, one can lose the points that make the difference between being funded and being rejected.

Typically, for foundations, put together proposals that are ten double-spaced, typewritten pages. Assume a half-page of introduction, a page of problem or needs statement, a page for goals and objectives, two pages for the plan of action, a page on your organization's qualifications [including key personnel], a page for budget and another for budget explanation, a page for project dissemination and continuation after the grant period. Do not overload the appendices to compensate for limitations on the proposal page length. Think about your reaction to a several-inch thick funding proposal when the "Request for Proposals" called for a 10 to 15 page proposal.

Proposals to corporations rarely should exceed five pages. Thus, write the ten page proposal for a foundation and wield a merciless red pen, cutting down every possible section, paragraph, phrase, and word. Brevity is a tremendous asset in the corporate world; if you do not demonstrate your appreciation of this, you will have greater difficulty interesting that corporate official in your proposal and project.

Proposals to U.S. Government agencies and programs are usually longer, but seek to limit your proposal to twenty-five to thirty-five pages. Some federal grant categories will have a page limit; others may not have explicit page limits, but remember that really long proposals will numb even the most dedicated grant panelist.

3. The proposal should develop logically and the various parts of the proposal should fit together well. Ideally, write the proposal with enough time to set it aside for a week or two. You will be amazed at the errors you will find and the corrections you will make with a little time between your first and second drafts!

NUTS AND BOLTS STRATEGY:

4. Finally, proofread, if you have time ask a colleague to review, and *do a second draft*. Remember, competing agencies, organizations, institutions are very serious about seeking funds from the same funding source you are approaching. It is a very serious competitive process. You must make the same good effort and demonstrate the same technical precision to ensure that your very good cause and your very good idea wins. Again, let's think about that college term paper. If you wait until the last minute to write the proposal, the proposal will read as if you wrote it at the last minute. But finish a good draft a week or ten days ahead of time, set it down, come back for a final review a day or two in advance of the required submission date and you will catch a lot of flaws—items you may have omitted, awkward phrasing, etc.

We admit our admiration for word processing software, but even the best programs can miss simple errors. Spell checking programs may miss words that are spelled correctly but are wrong ["there" instead of "their" or "they're"] and even grammar programs can make mistakes in checking more complex sentence and paragraph structures. So be your own checker, although you should take advantage of these programs. You may wish to activate the grammar check on your software and see how your writing registers on the Flesch-Kinkaid grade level and Flesch readability ease scale. These two related scales measure the simplicity or complexity of your sentence structure. On the one hand, you want to express somewhat more complex thoughts than "See Spot run; See Dick follow" but you also don't want to employ such turgid prose that the reader becomes lost in your complicated syntax, gives up, and grades your proposal down even though s/he probably won't admit that was the reason for the lower score. Consider writing somewhat akin to a tennis match—you want to vary the pace. Alternate some long, perhaps more complex sentences with some shorter, more simple ones—and the same with paragraphs. Try not to overuse certain words or phrases, e.g., "however," "paradigm," and anything else that smacks of an effort to overcome poor writing style.

First, you need to introduce the problem or need and the entire proposal. Write for a very intelligent yet not particularly knowledgeable reader. The grant evaluators are extremely intelligent people; after all, they are evaluating your proposal. However, you cannot and should not assume that they have any particular knowledge of your explicit problem and proposal. Try to write a brief introduction [perhaps at most a paragraph for a corporate proposal to half a page for a foundation proposal to two pages for a U.S. Government agency proposal] that defines the issue, challenge, or need in general terms, perhaps with an historical illusion, and then bring the discussion to the particular issue or challenge you wish to address. If you are, for example, addressing the issue of minority student attrition and retention, you could make introductory comments about the continuing role of education in American society, the general trends that concern you, and then the specific subset in which you intend to intervene. Include specific information—charts, graphs, data, and reports—drawn from your service area—a newspaper perhaps?—to help strengthen your argument. And be specific, for a problem on the West Coast might not be a problem on the East Coast; an appropriate concern in the Midwest might not matter in the Southwest . . . or even across a large metropolitan area.

An Example: Throughout American history, education has been and continues to be a source of upward mobility for successive waves of immigrants. Sadly, that rich legacy of educational and economic mobility is being threatened by an emerging trend in the Small City metropolitan area. Too many young people in our community are growing up in single parent homes; the feminization of poverty is a well-known phenomenon. The result is an increase in gang activity, a rise in teen-age pregnancy, children bearing and raising children, and greater numbers of high school dropouts.

However, a program devised at Medium Large City in a nearby state gives hope for mitigating these related phenomena by. . . .

Second, you need to describe the issue or challenge in a fashion that suggests the very reasonable response you are proposing. The problem cannot appear insurmountable; the issue cannot seem beyond the resources of the organization you represent.

Another Example: Teenage mothers are caught in a vicious cycle that threatens to trap themselves and their young children. Lack of affordable day care makes it difficult to complete schooling; inadequate financial support programs force many young mothers to enter the job market with inadequate or inappropriate job skills. Too many young children are forced to grow up quickly, to take care of even younger siblings, to do housework, and to become friends with their young mothers.

A recent series of reports in Our Local Daily Newspaper helps to highlight the problem. More than 80% of teenage women are sexually active; nearly 4% have children annually; social services agencies report a 35% increase in their caseload.

Although the problem is major and growing, the problem does suggest a possible solution, a way to reverse the trend, and thus to help save a generation and that generation's young children.

Third, you should describe your plan of action or methodology, providing appropriate detail and perhaps a time table to complement the plan of action. You should consider explaining why this plan of action or methodology is reasonable. There are many potential explanations: the organization has already employed it in other but similar projects; the approach has been used elsewhere and has been successful; a change may be needed from past practice; or some other justification.

Another Example: the nursing program at Local Urban State College requires that all nursing students undertake 150 hours of community service in their sophomore and junior years; the teacher education program at the same institution requires all students seeking teacher certification to perform 200 hours of community service. Local Urban State College proposes to use students in its human services program to oversee an outreach program that will provide young mothers with medical care, appropriate nutritional information for themselves and their children, and tutorial and mentoring assistance to complete their high school education.

The plan of action is simple and effective. Training will take place in the fall semester and a pilot project will commence in the spring term. Summer feedback will enable faculty overseeing the project to make appropriate revisions to expand the program in the fall of Year Two. And so on. . . .

Fourth, you should describe the results or outcomes you are seeking. That is, what will the funding source receive for its funds: a new approach to an issue of importance? valuable research? an improvement of a local community?

Another Example: the project proposes to improve the high school graduation rate among the target population of teenage mothers from its current 15% by an additional 5% a year until the graduation rate reaches 50% of the target population. The savings to society in reduced welfare, increased home stability, and improved health will outweigh by many times the modest cost of the project.

Fifth, you should describe your organization and explain why it is qualified to carry out the project you are preparing. Do not assume that external funding sources have either knowledge or, more important, accurate knowledge about your organization. Practice writing a good, solid paragraph or two of general organization description; this so-called boiler plate should go into every proposal. Then write several paragraphs about the specific qualifications of your organization in this specific project. You may need to refer to the section on Key Personnel; do so.

Another Example: Medium State Special Olympics [MSSO] was founded nearly thirty years ago to help state residents with mental and physical handicaps. Over the years, with a paid staff of only ten, MSSO has continually increased its services and the number of Special Olympians involved in programs. The expansion has been characterized by an increasing number of volunteers and increased fund-raising. However, a plateau of sorts has been reached that still leaves many potential Special Olympians without services. The proposal will enable MSSO to expand its services, reach the next level, and yet remain within the organization's capacity to oversee and manage the process.

Sixth, either in the plan of action, the discussion of organization capacity, or in a separate section, you need to discuss the plan of management. The plan of action discusses what you are planning to do; the plan of management demonstrates your commitment and capacity to overseeing the project. Having a committee meet regularly, for example, is not a plan of management; nor is having the proposed director report to an individual in the organization, although both may be part of a management plan.

NUTS AND BOLTS STRATEGY:

You can earn a lot of points if you have a good plan of management because too many proposals confuse the plan of action—what you are going to do—with the plan of management—how you are going to ensure that you do it and in timely fashion.

Even in a foundation proposal [e.g., only ten pages], you should have at least a paragraph, perhaps two, demonstrating how you will maintain project and fiscal integrity. Consider your current plans of management for ongoing operations and borrow the model for your proposal. Do not make the management plan onerous, but do make it effective and, as with any part of a grant proposal, "do-able."

Finally, you need to explain what will occur after the funding period ends. There are several approaches, and you may choose to use one or more of them. Some funding opportunities explicitly require you to discuss project continuation after the grant period; there is an expectation that your organization will continue the new initiative from its own funds or with funds generated from other sources. Depending on the project, you may wish to discuss that the next step is to take the project to the next level, and explain plans to expand, improve, or accelerate whatever it is that the organization is doing. Or, you may wish to discuss dissemination.

Example: the organization is committed to maintaining the project after the funding period ends. The grant budget has been construed on a declining basis—$40,000 in year one, $20,000 in year two, and $10,000 in year three—so that the organization will have to raise additional funds to compensate for the declining level of support from the grantor. It is a challenge, and the organization believes it can and must meet this challenge. To help fundraising, the organization will. . . .

Another example: the Coalition on Access for the Physically Challenged has planned a public conference to announce its findings of access in the downtown corridor. The mayor is providing funding for the conference. The result will be public pressure on business leaders and city council to consider and adopt recommendations of the eighteen month study.

C. Key Personnel

There are two issues that external funding sources will always consider: that your organization has the human resources and the organizational capacity to carry the project to a successful conclusion.

This section needs to demonstrate that there is an adequacy of human resources for the project and that each individual brings a needed skill, experience, or knowledge to the project. Simply appending resumes is not sufficient. The resumes probably do not deal specifically with the needs of your project; also resumes do not show the time commitment. You may wish to consider a narrative paragraph or page on each key individual [the project director having a little more description and other individuals having less], pointing out how their respective backgrounds qualify them for this project and also the percentage of time they are devoting to the project. Consider having your key personnel provide you with one or two page summary resumes directed at the project rather than full length resumes [or, for those in higher education, full curriculum vitae]. If you feel that complete resumes are necessary and that the grant competition will permit this, include them in an appendix.

In part, your funding source will determine the amount of material submitted in this section. For US Government grants, you very likely will need full resumes in an appendix; for foundation grants, a page or two for the entire section—that is, a paragraph at most on each of the key people—will suffice; for corporate proposals, you may have to keep the entire section to a long paragraph.

An Example: Jane Smith will be the Project Director, and will devote 50% of her time. Dr. Smith has served for six years as the associate director of the organization, and has directed several similar projects over the years. She has experience in working with at-risk youth and has published a number of articles in the area. [And then you could provide a sentence or two on the previous projects and perhaps a listing of one or two publications to demonstrate knowledge and capacity.]

Another Example: the organization proposes a team approach to dealing with the problem. Dr. Jim Doe will serve as team leader and project director on 50% released time. Each of the major social science and caring disciplines are represented: Dr. Doe [Psychology] and additionally Dr. Antonia Lopez [Human Services], Dr. Mark Williams [Social Work], and Dr. Mai Yi [Drug-Alcohol Abuse Services] all on 25% released time. [And then you would provide a sentence or two about their respective expertise: Dr. Lopez for many years has directed a combine college-church-community initiative to. . . .]

Yet Another Example: volunteers comprise a key personnel group for this project. Local State College has agreed to contribute the time of students for the project. Fifty Human Services majors will contribute some 100 hours each of their respective 200 hour community service requirement to the project over its 30 month life.

Of course, your description of key personnel should be more detailed, but there is no need in the narrative to exceed several pages for this section. Seek to convince the reader/evaluator that our organization has the necessary expertise to undertake the project and that key personnel can divide their time to meet current responsibilities and the new ones you seek to assume or that they can be released from [part of] their current responsibilities to assume the new responsibilities detailed in the grant proposal.

And, be reasonable. If your key person is so overworked that it is clear he or she will never be able to complete the tasks assigned, re-think the proposal. Or, if the key staff of the organization is so uninvolved, there is a different problem. The key personnel section should demonstrate both the quality of the people assigned to the project and their centrality to the organization's mission and functioning.

D. The Project Budget

The budget is a critical part of your proposal, and requires your close attention. In some ways, the budget may be the most important part of your proposal; grant reviewers frequently regard the budget as a key to the quality of the proposal. There are three considerations: you need sufficient funds to carry out the project; the funding source will want assurance that you are not "padding" expenses; and your own organization will need to know your internal [or, perhaps, "in-kind"] budget needs and commitments.

Most federal agency grant competitions have standard budget forms in their complete application packets. Even if you have to use such forms, consider including your own budget forms and budget narratives to define the project in your own terms. Set up the budget page with three or four columns across the page: category of expense, requested funds, matching funds from your organization, and, where appropriate [and possible], third party matching funds. Then have the following categories:

1. *Salaries and Benefits*: this category includes all the people involved in the project, including the project director and assistants, secretaries, students, volunteers, etc. If the organization is donating the services of individuals or if there are volunteers include the value of their work as the organization's matching contribution. Benefits are typically a percentage of salaries, and include such costs as retirement and health and life insurance. In terms of benefits, full-time employees on your organization's payroll will have higher cost of benefits—usually between 20 and 25% of salary—than temporary or part-time hires.

2. *Travel*: be realistic. Only account for necessary travel. Do not inflate this section to visit friends out-of-state or fly on a more expensive plane ticket. However, remember that meetings, site visits, and other forms of local travel can mount up—gasoline, auto depreciation, parking, etc.

3. *Equipment*: federal agencies, in particular, can be very sensitive to grantees seeking to obtain equipment that is not particularly germane to the project. Also, some grant competitions limit the percentage of grant expenses available for equipment purchases. Frequently, your organization is contributing equipment in-kind: desks,

file cabinets, chairs, tables, bookcases. Be sure to take credit for these contributions.

4. *Consultants:* consultants can perform valuable services in helping to analyze an issue, help with the project plan, and/or evaluate the project's outcomes.

5. *Supplies and Materials*: be aware of all the incidentals that go into any project; you need to account for such expenses as paper and pens, postage, telephone, printer cartridges, and more—unless you break out these items into detailed sub-categories.

6. *Institutional Overhead*: sometimes this is called "indirect cost recovery" [ICR]. Many foundations will not pay for ICR, and the organization will have to provide for its own overhead. Generally speaking, one or more federal agencies will negotiate an ICR rate for your organization; and many categories of federal grants have pre-determined ICRs—beginning at 8% for Department of Education raining grants.

NUTS AND BOLTS STRATEGY:

Finally, it is a good idea to have a budget narrative follow the budget. Take a sentence or two to explain each category, and why the need is appropriate for the project. For example, $10,000 for consultants may appear excessive, but a budget narrative might report an intention to have one consultant for personnel training, a second for mid-term [formative], and a third for final [summative] evaluation.

Here is a sample, completed budget:

Category	Grant Request	Organizational Match	3rd Party Funds
Salaries			
Director	$15,000	$15,000	0
Project Team	10,000	5,000	0
Secretary	7,500	0	0
Student Help	0	25,000	0
SUB-TOTAL	32,500	40,000	0
Benefits	6,500	8,000	0
Travel	1,500	1,500	0
Equipment			
Computer	0	0	2,500
Printer	0	0	500
Software	0	0	1,000
SUB-TOTAL	0	0	5,000
Consultants	4,000	1,000	0
Supplies/Materials	1,000	1,000	500
Overhead @ 8%	3,640	4,120	440
TOTAL BUDGET	$49,140	$55,620	$5,940

And a sample budget narrative:

1. *Salaries*: the coalition proposes to assign the assistant director of the center to the project full-time with salary divided between the grantor and grantee. The project team consists of five faculty from Nearby State University @ $1,500 per faculty per semester. The university will commit 250 students per year to help on a one-to-one basis with students at the middle school. The team will hire a college student to provide clerical assistance and data input for the project.

2. *Benefits*: are calculated at 20% of salaries [slightly higher for full-time personnel and slightly less for students].

3. *Travel:* is to compensate faculty team members and students for mileage from the university to the middle school at 20 cents/mile.

4. *Equipment:* the local computer franchisee is contributing an IBM Pentium 4 computer, a Hewlett Packard LaserJet Printer, and appropriate software as a third party contribution.

5. *Consultants:* the team wishes to bring a consultant to the training session for the college students, a mid-term formative evaluation, and an end-of-the-year summative evaluation to ensure the project remains on line.

6. *Supplies and Materials*: the team expects to spend the amounts noted on questionnaires and record keeping.

7. *Overhead:* is calculated at the allowable 8% ICR rate.

Some years ago, one of the authors, in his first big grant

proposal, devised a several million dollar proposal [to establish the first big endowment at that institution] to a major corporation in the state in which he was then living. He worked hard to devise a program, to make this program complement other programs already at that institution, and benefit from others at his institution, and to make a compelling case for funding the program. This was the early era of desktop based word processing programs and page maker programs, and the organization was proud of the resulting bound proposal that the president of that institution was prepared to present to representatives of the corporation in a meeting on the campus of the organization.

The meeting took place, with the corporation representatives on one side of a table and many representatives of the organization on the other side. There were overhead transparencies, the president practiced his remarks, and everyone was ready. Well, the corporate reps turned immediately to the budget—never mind all the proposal writing, and began questioning the entries! It was a budget for $100,000 a year for which the institution wanted a $2 million endowment [because, at a typical 5% payout, $2 million yields $100,000 annually].

[And, by the way, the president turned to the vice president who turned to the dean, and eventually they all turned to the far end of the table where the grant writer was sitting, and who explained how he arrived at the $100,000 a year annual expense budget; the corporate representatives were satisfied and eventually they funded the proposal through their corporate foundation.]

And the authors have sat on federal grant panels where the proposal received a generally good grade, but the reviewers pounded the budget, claiming it was padded, that institutional match was lacking, that there were expenses that could not be allowed, and so on and so forth.

There was a time when one of the authors sent a letter to several major national foundations inquiring about application guidelines for a proposal. He received several responses, and one check for $5,000.00. He had written in late November, and apparently the foundation in question operated on a typical calendar year and needed to spend 5% of its assets by December 31 to be in compliance with IRS rules, and apparently the foundation was about $5,000.00 short of compliance. Never discount dumb luck, but don't rely upon it!

Check your budgets carefully, for the proposed budgets really matter, and in some ways will determine the fate of your proposal more than any other.

E. Project Evaluation

As more and more prospective grant seekers compete for limited funding dollars, effective project evaluation becomes an increasingly important part of every grant proposal. For many years, foundations did not focus as clearly on this section. But outcomes are a key, and evaluation is the means to measure outcomes or change brought about by the grant.

There are many standard evaluation plans, but they fall into two basic categories: formative evaluation during the project to help refine the project and summative evaluation at the project's end to determine the project's degree of success. There are many ways to approach evaluation: use of external consultants, a survey of the target population [including "before" and "after"], a paired—T-test that compares the target population [or a subset] to a control group.

Example: the project will test the effectiveness of a delivery system with senior adults. The working group will consist of 100 seniors at 2 area senior homes; a control group of another 100 seniors at the same 2 area homes will be used for comparison [e.g., a paired T-test].

Another Example: pre—and post-project questionnaires will be distributed to the faculty, student volunteers, and middle school students to determine change over the course of the project [yet another comparison measure].

Another Example: Professor Terri Konoye of Downtown University will interview patients in the health care project; she will seek to measure improved knowledge of health care options and willingness to seek them out [i.e., summative evaluation].

Another Example: external consultants will review the project at six, twelve, and eighteen months; their reports will allow for regular review and revision of the project semi-annually [formative evaluation].

Now it is your turn. Quickly jot down a few ideas for evaluating your project. Remember, the evaluation should evaluate what you need to evaluate; this sounds silly, but many proposals fail because of inadequate evaluation plans or plans that fail to evaluate what the change the project promised.

F. Dissemination Plan

Many grantors want to know what the grantee intends to do upon completion of the project; usually this means either a dissemination plan or a project or a project continuation plan. Too many hastily-produced grant proposals gloss over the dissemination plan. The result is a loss of a point or two in proposal evaluation in a highly competitive process. Moreover, you should want to disseminate the positive results of your program [and the project will produce those positive outcomes, won't it?].

There are a variety of ways to disseminate outcomes. Here are several examples:

1. A press release to area newspapers and television stations;
2. A presentation of outcomes at a regional or national meeting;
3. A replication report available to other similar programs or organizations;
4. Perhaps a packet of materials for use elsewhere;
5. A local conference bringing together key members of the community;
6. Workshops to help groups, agencies, etc. affected by your study or project.

Sometimes, this section may include a discussion of the project after the funding period ends, although this discussion can also be included in the narrative or the evaluation sections.

Again, depending upon the grant proposal, you may wish to discuss project continuation. If the project had, as an outcome, the design of something for continued use, then use it. A faculty team may undertake a study to revise curriculum for teacher education or a social sciences program. A local non-profit organization may have studied its delivery system to test effectiveness. Whatever the design, project continuation would mean implementation of the design.

If the project needs to continue past the funding period, then a discussion of project continuation must include a discussion of continuing budgets. You may have applied to a local foundation for seed money and for continuation will look to a national foundation that typically makes bigger grants. or your organization may incorporate the project into its base budget. Regardless, the discussion of project continuation should be realistic to demonstrate you are committed to the project you are proposing.

G. The Abstract

Whether strictly required or not, consider writing a 100 to 250 word project abstract after you have completed the proposal. Here's why.

1. Many grantors, including federal agencies, publish annual lists of grants they made and use the abstracts in those lists. The funding agency will require you to submit an abstract and, perhaps, the proposal may fail technical review is there isn't one in the submission.

2. Smaller, local foundations frequently have their single paid professional staff present proposals to their volunteer board of directors; you have the choice of summarizing your program or relying on a busy, probably overworked professional to summarize accurately and favorably your program for presentation to the board. The more complete your proposal and the easier it is for the program staff to present your proposal the better your proposal will fare.

3. Abstracts are good tests. If you cannot summarize your program in half a typed page, then, perhaps, you are having difficulty in focusing on the proposal; perhaps the proposal is too broadly or loosely defined. If you cannot abstract your proposal, consider stopping RIGHT NOW and re-thinking what you are doing.

Abstracts should contain at least some of the following:

• The Title [preferably a "catchy" yet accurate title];
• Project Director and/or Principal Investigator;
• The Applicant: institution, organization, etc.;

- The Budget [including request and match];
- Project Time Frame [that is, beginning and end dates];
- Needs Being Addressed [especially how they fit the funding priorities of the funding agency];
- The Purpose of the Project [what you are going to do];
- The Method [how you are going to do it];
- Significance, Benefits, etc. [or why should the grantor be interested.

An Example: "Helping Children Help Their Children"

The Southside Neighborhood Coalition on Behalf of Children proposes to institute a pilot program to work with teenage mothers [and the fathers of their children] to improve pre-natal care, nutritional knowledge, raise high school graduation rates, and deliver improved day care. College students will work in a one-to-one peer mentor relationship with the group. Under the direction of Father James Clayton and Dr. Anita Glassman of Nearby State University, a project team will train college students to work with middle and high school expectant and young mothers through a variety of academic disciplines. The project cost is $85,000 over three years, of which the Coalition is seeking $52,500 in external funds. A longitudinal study of the group and a similar-sized control group will demonstrate the lasting effectiveness of the approach.

Another Example: "Creating a Pre-Service and In-Service Curriculum for Teacher Education Students"

Teacher State University is proposing a three year project to determine the effectiveness of Science Education in Elementary Schools, especially among teachers without a great deal of science education. The first year will be used to design survey instruments and other data collection means. The second year will gather and interpret data. The third year the team drawn from the sciences and teacher education faculties will design new courses for current teachers and teacher education students to introduce into the curriculum.

Now it is your turn!

H. Appendices

Appendices may include a variety of topics, including complete resumes of key personnel, a copy of an organization's [501(3)C] status from the Internal Revenue Service, newspaper articles, and an organization chart—just about anything. However, do not become carried away with appendices. Too often appendices add to the costs of producing a proposal without any benefit. Nonetheless, appendices do matter; it really is a question of balance.

The grant writer must consider the circumstances of the individual[s] reviewing the proposal. Many U.S. Government grant competitions bring together professionals from the field to evaluate the proposals in a brief span of time. Having to read, critique, and rate as many as thirty to forty proposals in four or five days, reviewers tend to appreciate proposals that are well done and complete but not longer than necessary. But there are always reviewers who want to know more.

Here are a few suggestions for appendices. Always test your appendices on the basis of their benefit to the proposal; if they are not needed, don't include them.

1. A brief description of your organization. Many institutions have a one page "fact sheet" that provides useful and accurate information about the organization. If your organization does not have such a sheet or brochure, you may wish to suggest one.

2. Information about your web site [which you should review regularly to ensure it is accurate and up-to-date.

3. A current organization chart, and perhaps a brief description of the positions on the chart.

4. A copy of the organization's non-profit status. Many foundations cannot transfer funds without proof from the IRS.

5. Favorable media coverage. If the coverage is related to your proposal, include some articles in an appendix.

6. Resumes of all key personnel [especially for federal grant competitions].

7. Additional data to support hypotheses and assumptions in the narrative. For example, the narrative may allude to statistics about aging; you may wish to include greater detail— e.g., national reports—in the appendix.

8. Course descriptions. In curriculum development proposals, the grant may have an appendix which lists existing courses related to the project and/or proposed new ones.

9. A map or maps. Some proposals involve working in the community or physically transporting people from one location to another. Offering a sense of physical space can be helpful to the grant panelists.

10. Summaries of previous, successful externally-funded projects. Success breeds success, and grantors like to go with winners. You may want to include one page summaries of previously successful projects.

11. Finally, letters of support belong in the appendices, but we shall discuss them in the next section.

I. External and Internal Letters of Support

A completed proposal can be a first rate idea; with time and commitment on the part of the grant writer and people who will be involved in project activities, the proposal can be very "do-able." However, grant reviewers want to see support for proposals within the organization and from groups in the community that will benefit from or will work with the project team to fulfill the activity. Lastly, experts in the field can provide a "reality check," that is, their expertise, for reviewers evaluating proposals.

Thus, the grant writer should seek to obtain letters of support. Internal letters are a must. If the project director, for example, is a faculty in a department, the grant should demonstrate support from the department chair, academic dean, chief academic affairs office, and perhaps even the president or even chief business officer.

If the project director works for a community-based organization, letters could come from the organization's leader and, depending on the size and scope of the operation, other key individuals.

Vague letters can be worse than no letters at all. Consider "assisting" your superiors and your supporters by drafting "sample" letters of support for their consideration. You then can make the points you want made and need to have in the proposal packet.

Appropriate external letters also are important. For example, if you are proposing a project in the community, letters from the mayor, key city administrators, and/or major individuals in the community all demonstrate that the project is well conceived and has broad support. You may wish to cultivate such people and keep them informed of your planning. Similarly, for federal grant competitions, you may wish also to seek support from your congressional delegation. Again, you may wish to "suggest" letters of support from these key leaders.

Letters from business leaders in your community also can strengthen a proposal. Business leaders are interested in the welfare of their community; letters of support that show their knowledge of and support for the project may gain you extra consideration and could result in a favorable funding decision.

Your turn: why not practice drafting several sample letters of support.

A sample external letter of support:

Dear Foundation Officer:

I have been asked by the Eastside Private-Public Partnership for Improved Schools to write a letter of support; I do so gladly, because, as the CEO of Large Corporation and as past President of the area Chamber of Commerce, I see great need for this project.

As you know, school dropout rates in the southeast side of our city are depressingly high and increasing; the problems are many-fold, but the primary causes relate to a breakdown of family and support groups.

The proposed project seeks to establish a mentoring system, working relationships with various businesses, and a series of safe houses to protect our children.

As the CEO of Large Corporation, I am committing this company to support the project as follows: we will provide mentors, summer jobs, and office support. Further, I will work with the Chamber of Commerce to convince other local businesses to support this project.

Your support in the amount of $35,000 over three years will provide the critical margin for this project, and demonstrate the tremendous commitment this entire community has to save our children and improve our community.

Thank you.

Sincerely,
Robert Jones, President

Another Sample Letter of Support:

To Whom It May Concern:

I am writing a letter of support for Private Liberal Arts College and its proposal on "Humanities Across the Curriculum." As a Professor of Humanities at Famous Private University, I have many years of experience in curriculum development and faculty development projects. I have much experience in the area of this proposal.

The project is well designed. The institution has an effective plan of operation and a plan of management. The budget is reasonable, no category is excessive, and institutional match is both significant and appropriate. The use of consultants throughout the grant period is particularly effectively designed.

*Equally important, the project is timely. The past
quarter century in American higher education has
witnessed an increasing departmentalization of the
curriculum; in some cases, scholars from different disciplines
cannot discuss a common topic because of disciplinary
differences in methodology and language. How can we
expect our students to negotiate these chasms? This project
is designed to help faculty converse across their disciplines,
then to modify the curriculum to help students gain a
more holistic approach to discovery and investigation.*

*I urge your strongest consideration of the proposal.
Thank you.*

Respectfully,
Professor John Q. Smith

J. Obtaining Internal Authorization

Every proposal for external funding needs internal
approval before submission to a funding source. Many
organizations, especially in higher education, have formal
internal authorization processes. Be sure to leave enough time
for the internal review process prior to the submission
deadline. If someone in your organization [other than you]
has responsibility for grants and sponsored programs, consult
with this person as you develop the proposal. If you intend to
commit any organization resources [including your own time],
you will need internal authorization.

More important, you want internal support for the project
you wish to undertake. There are several reasons: to protect
yourself, your organization, and the grantor, you need to
demonstrate that support exists internally for the proposal. This
support includes but is not limited to any promise of internal

"cash" or "in-kind" contributions, the released or transferred time of any organizational employee, the use of space and equipment, etc.

Failure to obtain such written, formal, internal authorization can lead to disaster. The grant may be funded, but institutional support does not exist. Or, at a key juncture in project activities, the project cannot obtain the support it needs [and promised the grantor it would have].

There is also a positive side. An appropriately completed internal authorization form helps inform major organizational constituencies—your work colleagues—about the nature of your project, the benefits to the institution, and other such matters.

The internal authorization form should include:

1. The project title;
2. The project director and/or principal investigator;
3. A project summary;
4. Time line[s] for the project;
5. A budget summary
6. Internal commitments [financial, personnel, space, etc.];
7. If the proposal involves human subjects, does your organization have a policy, committee, etc., to review such projects? If not, [please as soon as possible call a nearby college or university Department of Psychology and ask for a copy of APA Guidelines on Human Subjects Review.
8. Ditto the above for hazardous waste and its proper disposal?
9. Ditto for dealing with and taking care of animals?
10. Approvals: the head of the department, program, or office that will directly oversee the project, and then each administrative superior to the final authorizer—

perhaps the head of the organization, perhaps a senior business officer, perhaps a contracts and grants officer. Include this form in your proposal submission.

There is an example of an internal authorization form in the appendices. Please personalize it to fit your circumstances and your organization.

IV. Post-Writing Phase

A. *Producing the Proposal*

The final proposal document [and all the required number of copies] should be readable, clean, and with easy-to-identify sections. Avoid documents that are too fancy or slick. Veteran grant reviewers can tell stories of proposals that made a desperate case for support, pleading a lack of institutional resources. However, the proposal was expensively produced. Modern computer hardware, software, and peripherals make this easy and tempting, but avoid too much flash.

You should consider submitting the entire packet with a cover letter from the head of your organization [which you should draft]. This letter can be brief, but its inclusion signifies that you have your organization's support.

We are assuming that you have followed guidelines on the production of the proposal and submission deadlines. If you have failed to do so, especially if the deadline has passed, save the proposal for the next funding cycle. There are no rewards for late submissions. Why advertise that you cannot follow deadlines; apply early in the next funding cycle!

A rather minor point: sometimes, especially with federal grant competitions, the submitting organization must be able to demonstrate that it postmarked the proposal b y the deadline. Be sure to mail the proposal at a post office and not a self-service station or a drop box and consider asking the postal service employee to hand stamp the date [and even the time] on the cancellation.

Be sure to produce more copies than the minimum number required for the grant sub mission. Foundations sometimes only want an original copy; federal grant competitions will require an original and up to ten well-produced copies. However, you will want at least one complete copy for your files, for your administrative superiors, and for all members of the project team, and perhaps a couple of extra copies for unforeseen distribution needs.

B. How Grants are Reviewed after Submission

Do not be discouraged if your proposal is not funded the first time you submit it. Review panels can vary in composition from year-to-year and funding initiatives can change. A "hot" topic one-year can cool the next. Commitments from prior years and ongoing projects, in case of foundations, decreased income owing to downturns in stock markets, and for corporations, declines in the general business cycle all can limit dollars to distribute in a given year. But, if your proposal is not funded, write [or call] to request comments. Federal agencies will make available either comments or summaries of these comments. Foundations usually will only given oral responses; professional staff rarely have time to produce written critiques. Corporations have no consistent pattern. Use them for a thoroughgoing review to strengthen the proposal for resubmission.

Once the proposal is received, the funding source frequently engages in a technical review to ensure that the proposal meets the specifications of the category. Many proposals fail this technical review.

Thereafter, proposals are evaluated in several relatively standard ways. In the case of most foundations, especially the smaller, local foundations, the proposal may be summarized [remember the abstract!] and then presented to the review panel. Foundations use boards of directors to review proposals that the professional staff presents. You should seek to work with a member of the professional staff, i.e., a program officer, to discuss the submission of your proposal. The program officer is a key individual. He or she will summarize your proposal for the board [remember the importance of your abstract] and his or her level of interest and involvement will help determine the response of the board.

Federal agencies use panels drawn from the field in which you are submitting the proposal. These reviewers are, in a very real sense, your colleagues, and are very knowledgeable individuals. Typically, an agency or program brings reviewers together for a day [the National Endowment for the Humanities] to a week [the U.S. Department of Education]. Sometimes, however, an agency or program may mail proposals to reviewers to review at a distance and provide critiques for professional staff to evaluate.

After introductory comments, the reviewers begin reading and evaluating proposals typically in teams of two or three. At the end of the review period, again from a day to a week, the reviewers submit their written and scored evaluations. Agency program officers will adjust or normalize the raw scores from the reviewers and compare the sub-panels and then produce a list of proposals recommended for funding. Some individuals tend to rank all proposals high and others rank low, so agency officers adjust the range of scores to ensure that the best proposals in each sub-panel group are similarly scored. From time to time, these reviewers want to complete their assignments quickly to enable them to visit program officers for their own grants or to discuss future proposals with officials or perhaps with aides from their Congressional delegations. Clearly written proposals that deal explicitly with evaluation guidelines fare better in these kinds of evaluation processes.

Corporations vary widely in their review processes, so work closely with the respective public affairs offices. Frequently, a key and often unspoken concern is the direct benefit to the company from funding the proposal.

In each case, once the funding organization reviews your proposal and reaches a decision, it will contact you.

C. If the Proposal is Approved

"Congratulations" comes the telephone call or the letter. Take a moment and celebrate, for you have beaten the odds. Typically, funders turn down from four to seven proposals for each one they fund. Having celebrated [briefly!], you have two tasks before you, one minor and one rather major.

First, write appropriate expressions of gratitude and appreciation. You should call and/or write the funding source to thank it for awarding your proposal and to establish procedures for obtaining the funds, providing required reports, and other obligations. Be sure to thank all the people who assisted you—the project team, your organizational superiors, external supporters, etc. A little note, perhaps a small gift, or even a small reception [obviously **not** paid with grant funds] will make clear you valued all the assistance you received and should help you gain support for future grant proposals.

Second, run the project. The grantsmanship process put you in a position to carry out the project that caused you to seek a grant in the first place. So, set the grant-funded activity into action:

1. begin the respective plans of operation and management;
2. meet with the project team to firm the timetable;
3. meet with your organization's fiscal officers to set up the budget and appropriate budget controls;
4. meet with external or community groups that are involved in the project;
5. do all the little tasks that are necessary for success— paper, pencils, forms, office space, storage space, etc.;
6. you should consider a press release or informing the local media of the successful grant submission, and then keep them informed at key points in the project—you may generate favorable media coverage—and help your dissemination plan;
7. and, begin!

The hardest work is before you. Do a good job and good luck!

D. If the Proposal is not Funded

In a first submission, there is a strong possibility that you will receive a letter indicating your proposal was not funded. Do not be discouraged; this happens. Failure to fund the proposal does not mean necessarily that your proposal was bad. Instead, other proposals may have been more compelling or perhaps your proposal had a flaw that the reviewers simply could not overlook in a highly competitive evaluation process.

As soon as possible, contact the funding source. With a federal grant, ask for copies of the reviewers' comments; after you have reviewed them, speak with a program officer. If you applied to a foundation, call the staff to see where and how you can improve the proposal. If you applied to a company or state agency, try as best you can to obtain useful feedback.

With these evaluations in hand, you face a decision: to reapply or not. If the case for the need you indicated still pertains, then reapply. You may also wish to re-consider whether you should seek outside assistance, although you will have to pay for such assistance.

Perhaps you need to review the proposal development process. Did you provide enough time for a thoughtful process? Did you make your case clearly and specifically? Did you consult with a program officer for the funding source? Did you demonstrate your organization's capacity for the project? Its expertise? Did you select an appropriate funding source and submit an appropriate proposal?

Look at the proposal as a reviewer, and try to find where you can improve. Study with care the agency's guidelines, your budget, and your project management plan.

Regard this re-review as a beneficial step towards your overall goal. If you can find a weakness, if you can strengthen the proposal, then you are strengthening the project, helping to ensure its ultimate success, and that is a very good investment of time.

As the old saying goes, if at first you don't succeed, try, try, again!

E. Why Proposals are not Funded

Regardless of the comments you may receive from the granting agency, reconsider your proposal. Here are some common reasons why proposals fail.

1. You submitted the proposal after the deadline date;
2. You did not follow guidelines, and thus the proposal failed technical review;
3. The proposal did not fit a funding priority for the year;
4. The proposal was unimpressive; given the competition, your proposal did not appear original, compelling, etc.;
5. Some part of the proposal was not clear or complete, and this weakness in turn weakened the overall proposal;
6. The proposal was overly ambitious in terms of organizational capacity;
7. The proposal did not fit together: the solution may not have met the problem you indicated, or the budget did not reflect the solution;
8. The proposal was not sufficiently knowledgeable about the problem or the challenge or solutions being implemented elsewhere;
9. The proposal did not make the specific case for your community, organization, or institution. That is, the information you provided and the proposal you made were too general;
10. The budget appeared excessive, particularly the budget tried to shift general organizational operating costs to the project;
11. The organization's financial commitment was insufficient;
12. The proposal lacked an effective evaluation or project management plan;
13. There was no discussion or plan for project continuation after the funding period ended;
14. The proposal in general was sloppy—writing, production, etc.—and the reviewers were concerned that this may indicate sloppiness in the organization.

There are many other reasons, but these are some of the most typical ones for failure to receive funding. Take a long and honest look at your proposal to see if it falls into any of these categories.

V. Appendices

Quick Checklist/Forms

At the beginning and end of a project, it is useful t do a quick review: are you commencing the project properly? Have you completed it properly? To assist your efforts to keep the project on time and on-target, here are several quick forms—some of which we noted earlier.

1. A Project Budget

2. Internal Authorization

3. A Worksheet/Timeline—putting together a funding proposal involves a variety of tasks and commitments, and it can be useful to keep track of the tasks, to whom they were assigned, and due dates on a master form.

4. Review of "Do's" and "Don'ts"—the more you do correctly and the less you do incorrectly, the more likely you will produce a fundable proposal. Take a quick look from time to time and especially if the proposal is not funded and you wish to revise and reapply.

Typical Budget Form

gory	Grant Request	Organizational Match	3rd Party Funds
ries			
)irector			
'roject Team			
iecretary			
itudent Help			
)ther			
iUB-TOTAL			
efits			
el			
ipment			
:omputer			
'rinter			
ioftware			
iUB-TOTAL			
sultants			
plies/Materials			
rhead			
'AL BUDGET			

Internal Authorization Form for Proposal Submissions

Worksheet/Timeline for Grants

Over the years, I have found it valuable to have a worksheet, listing the tasks necessary to complete a grant proposal. As each task is completed, I can mark it and move to the next one. I also like a worksheet with a timeline, so that I can see if the project is moving at an appropriate pace; if not, perhaps a discussion on submitting the proposal at the next deadline date is in order.

Each group—non-profit organization, K-12 school or district, or higher education institution—should design its own worksheet. A more complex organization, for example, may require longer lead-time for internal authorization. A more complex proposal, for example, may have more parts, and thus also would require more steps and more time for completion.

Distribute an updated worksheet to all members of the proposal development team, and perhaps your administrative superiors. Let them all know the progress of the grant, and, perhaps, any difficulties you have encountered. Use the worksheet as a means to keep key individuals informed of the status of the grant.

These caveats notwithstanding, here is a sample; please design your own:

Sample Worksheet/Timeline

Date Done	Time Until Submission	Assigned To	Task or Assignment
	Anytime	Entire Unit Unit Head	Strategic Evaluation
	Anytime	Unit Head Committee	Needs Assessment
	Anytime >month early	Project Director	Plan of Action to Meet Need
	Anytime >month early	Grants Director	Finding Funding Prospects Gov't, Fdn., Corporation
	Draft at least Month prior To submission	Project Writer	Proposal Text Budget Internal Authorization
	One week early	Project Director	Making Copies and Mailing

"DO'S"

As a quick review, here are some "Do's" to help ensure an increased success rate for your proposal submissions.

1. **Do** begin your grant proposal by reviewing your operation.

2. **Do** leave enough time for a proper proposal development process.

3. **Do** include a great many people—all appropriate and useful people—in your proposal development process. Your proposal will benefit greatly from their expertise.

4. **Do** read the entire "Request for Proposals" or "Proposal Submission Guidelines" however it is titled.

5. **Do** read local newspapers and national newsmagazines; keep a clippings file of interesting ideas, good quotations, and useful data.

6. **Do** consider using the Internet to help you find useful information on topics of interest to you, on possible funding sources, and on what other similar institutions are doing elsewhere.

7. **Do** write regularly. The more often and the more pages you write, the better you will write, and, as a consequence, the better the final proposal.

8. **Do** consider a course in grantsmanship if you are expecting to author many proposals. Many local colleges, universities, and continuing education organizations offer reasonably priced [short] courses in grantsmanship.

9. **Do** demand institutional awareness and support for your proposal.

10. **Do** seek all appropriate institutional review of the proposal.

11. **Do** thank everyone for helping you, and do remember that you really needed his or her help.

12. **Do** think about partnering, bringing together support of various kinds from various funding sources to improve your chances of funding success.

DON'TS

1. Don't make the search for funding for a new project more important than your organization's regular operations.

2. Don't engage in a hasty process with a hastily done proposal. Wait until the next funding cycle.

3. Don't overlook or ignore proposal guidelines; you may fail technical review.

4. Don't omit a section of the proposal; reviewers will zero in on the omission and downgrade your proposal.

5. Don't forget to keep your superiors and colleagues informed.

6. Don't pad the budget; reviewers especially focus on budgets.

7. Don't forget a realistic institutional "match" on budget; the degree of "match" to some extent indicates the degree of institutional support.

8. Don't submit the proposal late.

9. Don't submit the exact same proposal with the same total budget to more than one source; let's be ethical.

10. Don't make a mass mailing—target your proposal to an appropriate source; don't waste time of funding sources that would not be interested in your proposal.

11. Don't "accept" and don't be discouraged by a rejection letter; don't pout: reapply!

12. Don't believe that a successful project submission is the end of your efforts.

SECTION III:

Nuts and Bolts:

The "Little" Things

"The Difference between success and failure is the difference between doing things right or nearly right"

Section III: Doing the Little Things Right

Let's begin by agreeing that donors and grantors do not give money in order to receive recognition. They support your cherished activities because they believe in your organization, they believe in your project, and they believe in the outcomes you are proposing to accomplish. You have helped them develop that sense of "buy-in," but that sense is very real and it is the key reason for their support. This is true whether you are discussing annual campaigns, local drives, formal grant proposals, or foundation inquiries.

However, in addition to two of the main purposes of this book—helping you to develop and strengthen your organization and helping you to find money to expand operations, improve what you are doing, or to extend the services you provide—we also must discuss how you do your public functions to thank supporters, your private appreciations, and your expressions of gratitude. Years ago, courtesy and politeness were the language of strangers, and there is something to be said for being courteous and polite, for thanking where appropriate, and for recognizing how important your supporters are to the success of your organization. It shows respect, and that you understand and appreciate the importance of their support. That is, your grandmother was right! [And don't you wish you had listened to her better!]

Before we begin, there is a caveat, well, actually, a series of related caveats. Let's get them out of the way first, and then we'll discuss how to show your appreciation. These caveats are very real, and you need to keep them in mind as you think about expressing appreciation.

In general, any appreciation should be limited. That is, you are not seeking and, indeed, not competing for financial support in any fashion simply to spend scarce and valuable funds on functions to thank the individuals and organizations that gave you that support. Thus, however you choose to express your gratitude, there have to be limits! And, for some organizations, there can be very real limits. Government officials frequently have limits on "gratuities" they can accept, and it is very important that you learn about such rules for local, state, and federal officials where you are located. You also more generally want to seek to limit such spending and spending on administrative or organizational overhead so that the percentage of each dollar given to your organization and spent on operations exceeds the average for the kind of organization you represent—be it K-12 school or system, higher education institution, or non-profit organization. That is, you want potential supporters to know that their support of your organization will result in measurable, programmatic improvements, not in nicer offices, fancier equipment, or, perhaps worst of all, really upscale parties.

Before we discuss social functions, let's pause for a moment for a refresher discussion on etiquette. Again, your grandmother was right! Remember to write "thank-you" notes promptly and be truly appreciative for the gifts you have received. If you intend to host public functions, you need to be sure that you and key members of your team have good public etiquette skills.

Remember to be neat and clean [maybe keep a bottle of mouthwash in your desk drawer!], to practice appropriate dining etiquette, to limit alcohol intake if you are, indeed, serving alcohol, and to remember why you are holding the event in the first place. That is, practice the etiquette skills you learned when you were young: greet people appropriately, make good eye contact, practice good body posture, shake hands well [all the way to the "webbing"!], don't speak with your mouth full, circulate to welcome all your guests, be careful what you eat and drink, don't be too loud, too insistent, or too dominating in conversation, and so forth. These may seem like very small items, but communications theorists have shown that most people draw lasting impressions in the first several minutes, and, if the image you accidentally project is not consistent with your organization, that negative image and message can cause you long-lasting damage. There are many books and nowadays many good web sites where you may review your public etiquette skills, practice them, and make sure that you are comfortable representing your organization in such public forums.

Some examples:

> Oscar Wilde noted: 'The world was my oyster but I used the wrong fork!'
> or, the chairman and CEO of a major, Ohio-based Fortune 500 company would ask his new hires about eating an artichoke—and usually they would have no clue nor would they know how to ask for help.
> or Henry Ford refused to hire management who salted food before tasting it. If they could season food without tasting it first, they might reach decisions without studying the issue of consulting with their colleagues and subordinates.

So, you may wish to eat one day looking into a mirror—
do you chew with your mouth closed? do you rest your
elbows on the table? do you take too large mouthfuls
when you eat? do you lean over your plate or do you
regularly spill a little of your meal onto yourself? do you
dominate conversations or let others speak? do you speak
with the persons on both your right and left? do you
keep your hands down [as opposed to gesturing broadly
and perhaps accidentally hitting the individual sitting
on one side of you]? It would not hurt to practice your
manners, because the key people you want to befriend
in your community probably practice theirs!

An aside: studies of corporate presidents and those who
sought but were never appointed president note that,
among other differences, corporate presidents have better
public manners. Learn to match their level of public
etiquette and you will do better in dealing with them.

Nuts and Bolts Strategies:

1. Thank you notes.

You need to think about standard "thank you" letters for
supporters and donors.

First, the IRS will require that you provide donors [whose
gifts were valued at $100.00 or greater] with a letter
indicating whether or not the donors received any goods
or services for their donation [and thus affecting the
amount of donation they may deduct from their corporate
or individual income taxes]. Typically, such donors have
not received any value, and need your letter for tax
purposes.

Second, you want to acknowledge the support of others. Think about some thank you notes—perhaps rather brief for small donations and perhaps more expressive for larger donations. Consider also being creative. But, most importantly, insist on timely acknowledgement of all gifts, because you can never say "thank you" quickly or frequently enough.

> For example, if your organization deals with young children, maybe the kids can paint or color cards you send out. Or it might be nice to have a thank you note that features a photograph of the children playing on the new equipment or in the new center or performing the new skills all of which resulted from the donations for which you are expressing appreciation.

> Consider the language of the thank you note. For big donors, consider the idea of "investments," and thanking them for their investments rather than their "donations." They are part of the team, and their investment is key.

Here are several sample thank you notes; again, and as your grandmother told you, responding quickly is better than responding late and never forget to express appreciation. That is, set up a system that once a week or once every two weeks, every donation that arrived in that time period receives causes a note to be generated. Set up a data table, and enter when the note goes out to ensure that you actually sent the note. Some 40 years ago, Bill Veeck, who used to own the Cleveland Indians and later the Chicago White Sox, wrote a great book, *Veeck as in Wreck*, and noted that to increase attendance the best payback came from encouraging those people who went once to go see a second game in a given season. The same holds true with donors—you are more likely to receive an additional donation from someone who already shares your values and believes in your mission than to receive a donation from strangers who you have to approach in the first place. Treat your current donors well, and you will be rewarded in turn.

A basic thank you letter:

Date

Dear So-and-So:

Thank you for your gift of [fill in the amount] to the Animal Association of Greater Small Town. Your kind gift will help us feed the animals in our care and to provide them with medical treatment until we can arrange for their adoption. It was so good of you to support our activities, and our silent friends also appreciate your support.

As you know, the needs of these unwanted animals exceed our ability to provide for them. Should you find that you can provide additional support, we would deeply appreciate your continuing generosity.

Thank you.

Name of Director

A more effusive letter to recognize a larger donation:

Date

Dear Mr. and Mrs. Smith:

Thank you so much for your wonderful donation of $ [fill in the amount] to support the new Smith Science Wing at Rural Community College. Your magnificent gift will enable us to update our science facility which is some 35 years old, and provide modern equipment and lab space for our students. The result will be improved service to our community and students more capable of working in our local industries.

This is a transforming gift, and we want to thank you in a more public way. I will call you in a few days to seek to arrange for a formal ground breaking ceremony to which we will invite local leaders and the media. We want everyone to know how much your investment means to the lives and future success of our students.

For the record, and as the IRS requires, I am stating that you received no goods and services for this commitment to RCC.

Again, thank you, and best wishes for a healthy and happy fall season.

Sincerely,

Name of Director

2. Small expressions of appreciation.

You ought to consider small expressions of appreciation to thank individual donors, local companies, foundations, etc. This could mean purchasing some pens, coasters, pads of paper, or even T-shirts with the logo or name of your organization or project. I like the old fashioned western, on the range, coffee mugs emblazoned with one's logo or name and maybe some fancy coffee with a nice note about how that individual's support warmed us and we wanted to return the favor. Regardless of what small gift you choose, it's a nice way of saying "thank you" and it is also free publicity. Years ago, a basketball coach at an urban institution gave T-shirts with the college logo to all the young children who attended his free inner city basketball clinics; for years afterwards, driving through that part of this large, urban community, one could see elementary school age children running around the streets wearing those shirts—nice advertising! There are gift catalogs, and again many web sites and there are good discounts for purchasing in volume; it may be worth your time and effort to investigate some of them.

> You might be able to work with a local supplier and receive an in-kind donation to create these small give-away items. That is, perhaps the local supplier will give these to you at cost—T-shirts for $5.00 each or pens or pencils or pads for pennies apiece or little stress squeeze balls or small credit card-size calculators.

It is worth a thought, and you may wish to check what other similar kinds of organizations in your general area—K-12 school district foundations, higher education institutions, non-profit agencies—are doing and then devise something appropriate.

3. The annual appreciation dinner or reception

Please consider hosting an annual appreciation dinner or reception for good friends of your program. Keep the scope and scale of the event consistent with the program you lead. If, for example, you are the Director of a small non-profit organization, consider a reception for all donors who have given $100 or more that year and perhaps a dinner thereafter for donors who have given $1,000 or more. Establish limits and cut-offs with which you are comfortable—a dessert reception perhaps and not a dinner or a cookout rather than a fancy, sit-down affair, but you want to take time at least once a year to thank the good supporters who have helped you accomplish the good work you want to achieve. Remember, some supporters give cash, some gift their services, and others may gift their time or good name—all of which are valuable and you should be prepared to express your appreciation to all of them!

A. There are several steps involved in planning and carrying out a successful appreciation event.

1. First, you need to select an appropriate time frame, and this means checking the local calendar of events in your community. It would be silly, for example, if you are a small non-profit organization to select the same evening the your community's United Way or other major coordinating non-profit organization has chosen for its annual dinner or similar event. If you are a small private college in a community where there is a large university, you might not want to compete with the annual and highly regarded football match against its chief competitor. Check the calendar of events in your community early, and this may mean several telephone calls to the local chamber of commerce, the local school district [for back-

to-school nights, school assemblies, and such]
and perhaps some local churches or other
religious organizations. And, once you have
settled on a time and date, let some of these
groups know so you may have "first claim" of a
sort.

2. Once you have an appropriate evening, set up
   a backwards time line, so that you will then
   have a timeline to follow that will lead you to a
   successful event. That is, counting backwards
   from the date of your event, figure out how much
   lead time you need to ensure that each of the
   steps to organizing a successful event takes
   place in a timely manner.

   There are many steps, including putting
   together the guest list [ensuring proper spelling
   of the names of your guests], printing the
   invitations and mailing them perhaps three to
   six weeks in advance of the event; arranging
   for the facility [hopefully it is your own base of
   operations and thus you can show off what you
   do to your key friends in the community];
   ordering or preparing food and refreshments
   [for example, a caterer might need 3 or 5 days
   notice on head count for ordering food and for
   you to guarantee quantities]; making out name
   badges, printing programs, ordering flowers or
   centerpieces, arranging for music, and securing
   dignitaries or guest speakers.

   Sometimes you may be so fortunate to have
   volunteers to whom you can turn over much of
   this work, but please check on their progress

since, if something goes wrong or is not done completely or correctly, it reflects on your organization. Establish your time line, check it frequently, and make sure that all proceeds on schedule. There is something to be said for the way that construction engineers set up a flow chart for the constructing of new buildings, for example, and how they keep track of all that is going on so that one group of work people are not competing with another.

B. Practice a format for your invitations; they need not be excessively fancy—you can arrange to purchase at a stationary store some nice but simple invitation paper stock printed and reasonably standard envelopes. Draft some sample text and let some friends critique what you have written, consider having a contact person for additional information [name, phone, and today maybe even e-mail address], and for dinners or for events where headcount matters, include a date for responding. Here are a couple of sample invitations:

The Northside Coalition for Improved Schools
cordially invites you to
a reception in honor of
our new recreation facilities

Northside Softball Complex
Thursday, April 17, 200x
4:30—6:00 pm

R.s.v.p.   Jane Smith
555-1234
jsmith@ncis.net

or

The Small Town Schools Foundation
cordially invites you to
the opening of
our new computer lab

Small Town Middle School
Tuesday, October 12, 200x
7:30 am

For additional information: John Jones
555-4321

or

The Community Alliance for
Youth cordially invites you to
our annual dinner and awards ceremony

The Downtown Fancy Hotel
Main Ballroom
Thursday, November 15, 200x
5:30 pm—Reception
6:30 pm—Dinner
7:30 pm—Program

R.s.v.p.   Stephanie Johnson
555-1111
sjohnson@cayalliance.org

Select a nice typeface [I have always liked Zapf Chancery 14, by the way], pick appropriate paper, and work on the wording of your invitations. You must convey all necessary information. This may sound silly, but I have seen one organization that has real difficulty in its invitations letting potential guests know the date, time, and location of the event. Follow-up calls are not always returned, and so this lack of attention to detail takes the shine off the event before it is held.

C. Make the event fit your organization. If you are a small organization, consider a reception rather than a dinner. Perhaps one of your employees can play piano or violin or the harp or perhaps some of your neighbors have a small jazz combo and would be pleased to play. Sometimes you can rent flowering plants much cheaper than you can purchase cut flowers. You need to keep the spending and scope and scale of the event appropriate for your organization—its size, its operations, etc.

D. Make up your guest list, and think about it carefully. You should invite the people whose support made the project possible. You might want to invite people whose support you want to earn, to convince them of your organization and its community support. Finally, you may also wish to invite community leaders, just to let them have a sense of the good news about your organization.

E. Also consider who from your organization you think should attend the event, and then explain the purpose to them so that they can help with the unstated but needed goals of the event.

F. Check the guest list carefully; make sure that "John" does not receive a letter addressed to "James" and so on and so forth; ask for replies, and keep an accurate count—nothing can cause more trouble than to expect, for example, 16 people to dinner and 24 show up or to expect 250 at a reception and only 75 come. Ask those people taking the replies to ask for the names [and proper spellings] of all attendees ["thank you, and will you be bringing someone?"].

And consider asking about dietary restrictions. That is, if you really want to serve a heavy meal, perhaps some of your guests can eat such food or perhaps they are lactose intolerant or vegetarians or on salt-restricted diets. Either plan a menu that has lots of alternatives [a fruit tray along with heavy desserts for a reception; a dinner featuring chicken rather than roast beef or pork; a light hand on the spices, etc.].

G. Make up a data table with a little information about each of these key attendees [name, title, organization, nature of support or why s/he was invited] and make sure that your each member of your leadership team has a chance to review the table [e-mail it around a day or two in advance]; make up name tags or, for a small dinner, table place cards.

H. Be prepared to have a short program—typically the shorter the better—but do take time to express appreciation to your "difference makers" both outside and inside the organization—don't do one of those long winded "Oscar ceremony" speeches that drag on, but do quickly thank them and let them receive the acknowledgement of the folks in attendance.

I. No matter how big or small the event, no matter how large or limited the budget, make it quality. This does not necessarily entail money, but, rather, it means your own involvement. Aim for nice touches, be on hand to greet people as they arrive, let your staff know your expectations for their responsibilities that evening— this is an important opportunity and it only comes once a year! Make sure the program staff circulates, make sure every important attendee has "face" time with program officials or receives a guided tour to the new facility, or whatever.

J. Finally, and this item probably should be considered first, if you are holding an annual appreciation event, you need to consider are you "comping" everyone or are you charging most guests to attend. That is, is this a complementary event or are you viewing it as a money maker? It is a key question, and one you need to consider. Charging a reasonable amount per ticket certainly defrays costs—so if you are an on-going foundation or a continuing community agency, you ought to consider charging an appropriate amount which will help you arrange for a nicer event. If you are something new, and perhaps if you have engaged in your very first fundraising effort, you might want to arrange something modest in cost and free to all your guests.

"Genius is in the details!"

Let's pause for a moment for some real screw-ups that the authors have seen occur. Some examples:

> A public university wanted to thank donors for a newly endowed chair, and arranged for a dinner at the president's home. The foundation at that university

handled the arrangements—developing the guest list, sending invitations, collecting responses, and letting the president's house staff know the resulting numbers. The big day comes, and the president, his wife, and the special events coordinator—everyone!—is prepared for a dinner for 16 people. 24 people came to the dinner!

A dish featuring chicken breasts became a stir-fry featuring sliced chicken! And there was lots of salad! While the guests were having additional drinks in the entrance area, the kitchen staff was carrying an extra table from the kitchen, down the back stairs, through the yard, and then into the formal dining room and hurriedly setting that table to accommodate eight extra guests.

The next day it came out that the foundation distributed the invitation list around its office so that all the support staff could take messages from invitees; the individual who was coordinating the function failed to collect all the lists, and missed eight individuals, including the lead donor to the endowed chair!

and there was . . .

A good sized non-profit organization wanted to host an outdoor reception to thank supporters and to announce a new program. The late afternoon arrived, the weather was surprisingly pleasant, the crowd showed up, expecting a pleasant time, heavy hors d'oeuvres and beverages.

The business manager of the non-profit feared spending money, and so she had two wait staff individuals walking around two [yes, two] trays of food for more than 250 guests; there was one table for beverages on a hot late summer evening—again for 250 people.

As you should imagine, many of the invited guests walked away, commenting to one another that they had assumed they could make dinner out of the event, and they were leaving early because they were hungry. A golden opportunity lost!

and there was . . .

The Executive Director of a medium-sized non-profit organization was hosting a dinner at his home to thank his key leadership team—both paid staff and volunteers. The clerical support person who typed up the data table for the guest list had the third column [home addresses] one off from the first two columns [last names and first names] so, with the exception of the first individual, every other invitee's invitation went to someone else's address.

The resulting apologies for this unintended gaff more than negated the good will the event should have generated.

and there was . . .

The time a non-profit organization sent invitations that had the date and time but not the location for the social event,
  and the time the same non-profit sent invitations that had the location but not the date and time,
  and the business people on whom the non-profit organization relied upon for support drew conclusions that the organization was not as organized and not as

well run as it probably was—all because someone did not check the details.

and there was . . .

The time that a medium sized public university held an appreciation event and the external relations staff that planned the event did not brief the institutional President ahead of time who was attending. That is, they did not provide the President [and perhaps other key institutional leaders] with a simple data table indicating the guests, their affiliations, and their relationships, if any, to the institution. The President wound up spending much time with very nice people who, unfortunately, were not the key movers and shakers in the community, and a golden opportunity was lost.

and there was . . .

The time that another non-profit organization—and this happens all the time—held an appreciation dinner and the officers of the association [and their spouses and guests] all sat together rather than distributing themselves and the key volunteer supporters at every table to help make all guests feel welcome, and to gently publicize the organization, its successes, and its future goals.

and there was . . .

The president of a small private college wanted to host a reception and dinner for key donors at her home. As she and her assistant [who would be greeting guests at the door and helping with arrangements] left the office to go to the home just in advance of the guests' arrival, they

both realized the president had left her now-dry clothes
on the outdoor clothes line in the yard. Hurriedly, as the
president freshened up, the assistant grabbed the clothes
off the line and took them inside before guests arrived.

Simply put, social events are important, valuable, and take
time. If done correctly, they make staff feel valued; they make
supporters feel valued; they can make new friends. If done without
much detail or attention, they can set your organization back.

3. Announcements of Major Gifts, Grants, etc.

A. You should consider an appropriate announcement
of a major gift, grant, or other significant source of
funding and resources. People like to invest with
winners, and the fact that you have received one
significant source of funding can and will help you
obtain others. Consider a press release that you
would send to the major media outlets in your area
[which may be as few as the local newspaper and
the local radio station in a smaller community] and
also to the local chamber of commerce, the mayor,
and perhaps several selected business leaders. The
announcement should be brief—noting the funding,
its source [very important—give this credit!], the
project it is supporting, and the goal [and thus why
the community should be interested].

B. You may also wish to issue a brief press release on
the start of the program, and at important points
along the way [if there is truly measurable,
demonstrable progress] and, of course, at the end.
Keep copies of any of these releases, and if they are
printed in the local media, for example, keep copies
as proof of your dissemination plan to the funder.

C. If you received funding for a facility, consider a formal groundbreaking ceremony. If this is the case, consider renting a tent, purchasing some ceremonial shovels, arranging for a nice ceremony [which also is a nice photo opportunity perhaps on a slow news day in your community?!], informing the media well ahead of time, inviting key guests [including representatives of the funding source], etc. Arrange for some refreshments, hope for good weather, and have at it! As always, make sure that your remarks express appreciation to all those who deserve it, and consider letting the representative of the funding source speak. Make up a nice program—desktop publishing and all that. Do a nice job on the details, which would include name badges for key guests, a nice and simple program, some staff to help greet your key guests as they arrive, flowers, refreshments, perhaps some enthusiastic beneficiaries of the gift [thus, if it is a fundraising campaign for new recreation fields—have some children dressed in team uniforms come charging out, etc.].

4. Employee Appreciation

A. If either obtaining this special funding for a new or expanded program or a new or expanded facility that will assist your programming really meant that some people on your staff acted above and beyond the call of duty, consider a small token of appreciation—some kind of thank you that lets those good folks know that you recognize what they did and that you appreciate it. Grandmother was right: saying "please" and "thank you" does not cost much, and the returns can be great!

B. If your organization is big enough, here are some nice ideas that we are borrowing from others.

One Foundation President established a breakfast birthday celebration day each month. So, once a month, at a previously agreed upon date [e.g., the first Monday or the second Tuesday], he would treat all the staff whose birthdays fall in that month to breakfast at a local eatery. It is not that expensive, but a nice breakfast, taking some time to thank people for their good work—this all kind pay real benefits in terms of employee work effort. So you should certainly thank your staff for their good effort—a short handwritten note, for example, can work wonders and takes only a few moments to pen. You cannot say "thank you" enough—to your staff, to your supporters, to just about anyone and everyone. The more inventive you can say "thank you," the more memorable that recognition and appreciation will be.

Another non-profit President would arrange for an office pot luck and he would bring his special barbecue as the main course. Everyone was able to dress "down" since barbecue is messy, and the luncheon became a real team building opportunity.

Whatever you do, do what fits your personality, your organization's profile, and your budget—it is the thought, and not the cost that counts!

but you can go wrong if you aren't careful

One non-profit organization president would have a luncheon at the house for the support staff in the organization, telling them how much he appreciated their good work and how important they were to the organization's success. Then, when they would return to the office from the lunch, he would hand them the bills to process against the organization's funds. There was nothing personal about the luncheon, the secretaries were not comfortable in that situation, and a well-meaning and well-intended gesture failed.

C. Along the same lines, if you are in charge of a moderate sized organization, you will receive opportunities to attend events, to see ball games, plays, musical performances, to go to grand openings of exhibits, and much more. You personally should have to attend some of these events; but, for others, consider distributing the tickets or passes to your staff. If you have a secretary for whom baseball is a real treat [or maybe she wants to take a favored grandchild], and you receive some free passes to the local minor league baseball team or there is a program assistant whose passion is orchestral music and the local symphony is putting on a program, why not let that individual or those individuals attend, represent your organization, and have a pleasant evening out with a spouse or friend. I always like the organizational head who, at holiday time, in receiving a gift of food, puts it out in the "break" room and lets everyone have a snack—it's a morale builder!

One college President was a real baseball fan, and he lived in a town with a major league baseball team which, while popular, could not fill the entire stadium where it played for every home game. It would lease out some luxury boxes game by game rather than for the season. So this President leased the box, and invited everyone in the leadership of this institution to join him. While they had to pay the cost of the ticket [no more than a regular seat], they sat in a box, had a great time, and felt valued.

5. In-Kind Contributions Appreciation

A. One of the best kinds of support is "in-kind" support from local agencies and companies in your area. For example, the local newspaper might give you a reduced price or even free advertising for your event or your program; local suppliers might give you goods at their cost; others might donate their services and labor, which can save very real money, etc. Let's say, for example, that you have organized a reading program, and a local ice cream parlor or fast food outlet has donated to reward children who achieve the goal, please arrange a significant thank you to this important corporate contributor; perhaps you raised money to create new recreation facilities, and a local lawn and garden store either provided planting materials at reduced cost or arranged to plant them and donate the labor—thank them! The price reduction from full cost retail is a real savings and a real sign of support that you can use in your grant proposals as a third party match, and so you should thank them for the full value of that savings even if it does not cost that local supplier very much money. It can be saving you a great deal!

Libraries, for example, have frequently "connected" with local ice cream parlors and fast food establishments in promoting summer reading programs. If children read so many books they may receive a coupon for a free ice cream cone or a free sandwich and french fries. The library has a "bribe" to encourage the great habit of reading, and the local restaurant establishment builds good will and probably sells something to the parent accompanying the child!

B. The point here is really simple: you cannot say thank you often enough—write them a letter; or, depending on what the project is, consider having some of the recipients sign a letter. Imagine the power of a letter from a group of baseball or softball teams thanking a lawn and garden store or a local contractor or the Kiwanis who volunteered their time to clear the field or whatever—and they receive a nice thank you note from an appreciation group of children or perhaps an autographed team jersey or poster or baseball or basketball. Wow!

6. Check List of Do's and Don'ts

Finally, here are some simple Do's and Don'ts to keep in mind [some of which are repeating in bullet format items which we have discussed above].

A. You cannot say "thank you" enough;

B. Say "thank you" as if you mean it, because you should mean it—even if the same wonderful donor continually and regularly contributes to your cause and even if you don't need to make much effort to secure the donation, don't ever forget to say "thank you" in a meaningful and sincere way;

C. There are lots of people to thank—donors—both cash and in-kind, supporters in the community, your staff, and even the wonderful people to whom you are directing your services—thank them all;

D. Thank your supporters, friends, and colleagues in appropriate fashion;

E. Recall and, if necessary, practice the rules of etiquette—they have real value;

F. Spend time on planning any public functions—be they large or small, fancy or simple—so that the event proceeds very smoothly;

G. Think about dietary restrictions in your menu selection [if your guest list is older, you may want to be sure that dinner is low fat or dairy free or limited salt, etc.];

H. Remember to make up a backwards time line, like a construction schedule, to make sure you remember to do everything at the appropriate time—setting the date, ordering all that needs to be ordered, devising invitations, mailing them, collecting replies, etc.

I. Little touches at these events can make a real difference [nice name badges than are on a chain for women and with a clip for men—dresses vs. suit jackets instead of peel off name tags] in your guests' perception of these events;

J. Be visible at these events—CIRCULATE!—and insist your key personnel circulate as well;

K. After the event, you may still want to thank people—
significant guests who attended or perhaps those
individuals and companies who contributed
somehow to putting on the event [the florist who
sold flowers at cost, the caterer who provided dishes
for free, etc.];

L. Consider purchasing some small gifts—really tokens
of appreciation—that you can give to donors and
good friends as a visible reminder of your gratitude;
keep these gifts very reasonable in cost—it is the
thought and not the actual gift that counts;

M. Do something regular to thank your staff—a card on
a birthday, perhaps a once a month birthday
breakfast for all who have a birthday that month,
etc.—but do something above and beyond the
normal range of daily activities;

N. Make yourself and your agency known in your
community—work with the local media, let your
local government and business leaders know what
you are doing [appropriate press releases and
invitations];

O. Try and arrange for events that fit into the calendar
of community events and also help the local media
with their job of informing the community;

P. And, if you have a volunteer board [whether it is a
governing or just an advisory board], involve them
in all the planning, in speaking at events, etc.—
keep them involved, make them feel appreciated,
and use them as appropriate.

"People Types

and Tiger Stripes"

7. An Aside That May or May Not Be Helpful

The authors have a sense of what it takes to be a competent non-profit organizational director, the kind of culture an organization needs to be successful, the kind of values an organization needs to put on public events well, and the processes and skills it takes to be effective in fundraising and grantsmanship.

But, at a certain level, this sense reflects an awareness of and an appreciation for differences in human personality types. While we are not seeking to make believers in any one theory out of our readers, and while we are not comfortable arguing or insisting that you agree that people can be categorized as "this" or "that" personality, we do believe that effective leaders have an intuitive appreciation for differences in people. That is, the more you can understand and appreciate differences in people, the better your organization will function and the more success you personally will have in your leadership role.

If you agree, you might wish to purchase from your local bookstore or borrow one of several books from your local public library. I have always liked *Type Talk at Work: How the 16*

Personality Types Determine Your Success on the Job by Otto Kroeger and Janet M. Thuesen and also *People Types and Tiger Stripes* by Gordon Lawrence. Both books reply on the Myers-Briggs Type Indicator to help you understand yourself and others around you better. You may wish also to contact the Center for the Application of Psychological Type or peruse some issues of the *Journal of Psychological Type* since the MBTI is a registered product. If you are interested, the MBTI helps indicate differences in people that result from:

- where they prefer to focus attention;
- the way they prefer to take in information;
- the way they prefer to make decisions;
- and, how they orient themselves to the external world.

These differences can have real implications helping to determine your leadership style, the culture of your organization, and how you interact with key audiences, including the community leaders from whom you seek financial and other support.

1. Thus, some people focus on the outer world of people and receive energy from external events, experiences, and interactions; some people focus on their own inner world of ideas and experiences and receive energy from their internal thoughts, feelings, and reflections. That is, some people are energized by being with people, and others may be exhausted or need a rest period. You may wish to consider this in arranging, for example, for a visit from a key donor or donor prospect.

2. Some people prefer to take in information through their senses and are very observant of what is taking place around them; some people instead focus on the big picture, on the

connections between facts, and seek patterns and new ways of doing things. The first may not be comfortable seeing "the forest" while the latter may not particularly be interested in "the trees." You should realize that, for example, depending on "type," you may wish to change your approach to difference key corporate figures and/or potential donors.

3. Some people prefer to use thinking in decision-making and believe there is an objective standard of truth, while others make decisions on person-centered values seeking harmony and recognition of individuals. That is, some people care more about an objective standard while others care more about not hurting people—imagine, if only in terms of the annual evaluation, what a difference in approach these two types would have.

4. Finally, some people prefer to live in a planned, orderly way, make decisions, achieve closure, and move on. Others tend to live in a flexible, spontaneous way, and are open to last minute options.

And, as you would expect, most people are distributed somewhere along the broad line between these four sets of opposites.

You should already be nodding, recognizing how some times when you have made fundraising presentations the potential donor quietly listened, and perhaps took notes and other times the donor may have joined in the conversation. Indeed, some may have appeared to have had no reaction while others wound up dominating the conversation to the extent that you were unable to finish the presentation or make it as you had planned.

Some may have shown more concern with the details of the proposal, while others may have been concerned with the big picture, the goals, and the potential outcome. You need to be prepared for both situations, and, indeed, to anticipate that both may occur.

Some may have asked for an agenda ahead of time, perhaps in great detail, while others seemed far more "spur of the moment," caught up in the excitement of what your organization does and can do with greater support and new resources. Some may have wanted to read while others may have wanted to discuss.

If you want to be more conscious of the range of personality types and how that can affect your success and that of your organization, you may wish to arrange for a consulting visit from someone with this expertise, perhaps affiliated with the Center for the Application of Psychological Type [CAPT] or other, similar organization. Or, if you are not wholly sold, consider borrowing the books noted above from your local public library.

Regardless, the more you appreciate that people are different, and learn to pick up on those differences, the more success you will enjoy in leading your organization and in obtaining the resources the organization needs to do the good work it can and should do.

THANKS AND GOOD LUCK!

A Very Brief Bibliography!

Ultimately, there are many good books on all the topics that we have discussed. The key is the "fit" with you and your organization. Some books, some ideas, some approaches work better for some leaders and for some organizations and other books work better for other people. You may wish to peruse these books at your local bookstore or public library or on-line at such companies as Amazon.com. Good luck!

On managing non-profit organizations:

1. Stoesz, Edgar and Chester Raber. *Doing Good Better! How to be an Effective Board Member of a Nonprofit Organization.* Intercourse, PA: Good Books, 1994.

2. Upshur, Carole C. *How to Set up and Operate a Non-Profit Organization.* Englewood Cliffs, NJ: 1982, Prentice-Hall, Inc.

3. Bernstein, Leyna and The Management Center. *Best Practices: The Model Employee Handbook.* San Francisco, CA: 1998, Jossey-Bass Publishers, Inc.

4. Setterberg, Fred and Kary Schulman. *Beyond Profit: The Complete Guide to Managing the Nonprofit Organization.* New York City, NY: Harper & Row Publishers, 1985.

5. Allison, Michael and Judy Kaye. *Strategic Planning for Nonprofit Organizations: A Practical Guide and Workbook.* New York City, NY: John Wiley & Sons, 1985.

6. Wilbur, Robert H., editor. *The Complete Guide to Nonprofit Management. Second Edition.* New York City, NY: John Wiley & Sons, 2000.

7. Reiss, Alvin H. *CPR for Nonprofits: Creating Strategies for Successful Fundraising, Marketing, Communications and Management.* San Francisco, CA: Jossey-Bass Publishers, Inc., 2000.

On fundraising:

1. Stallings, Betty and Donna McMillion. *How to Produce Fabulous Fundraising Events: Reap Remarkable Returns with Minimal Effort.* Pleasanton, CA: Building Better Skills, 1999.

2. Flanagan, Joan. *Successful Fundraising: A Complete Handbook for Volunteers and Professionals.* Chicago, IL: Contemporary Books, 1991.

3. Warwick, Mal. *How to Write Successful Fundraising Letters.* San Francisco, CA: Jossey-Bass Publishers, Inc., 2001.

4. Mutz, John and Katherine Murray. *Fundraising for Dummies.* Forest City, CA: IDG Books Worldwide, Inc., 2000

On Grant Writing

1. Browning, Beverly A. *Grant Writing for Dummies.* Forest City, CA: IDG Books Worldwide, Inc., 2001.

2. Miller, Patrick W. *Grant Writing: Strategies for Developing Winning Proposals.* Indiana: Patrick Miller & Associates, 2000.

3. Burke, Jim and Carol Ann Prater. *I'll Grant You That: A Step-by-Step Guide to Finding Funds, Designing Winning Projects, and Writing Powerful Proposals.* Portsmouth, NH: Heinemann, 2000.

4. Robinson, Andy. *Grassroots Grants: An Activist's Guide to Proposal Writing.* Berkeley, CA: Chardon Press, 1996.

5. McIlnay, Dennis P. *How Foundations Work: What Grantseekers Need to Know about the Many Faces of Foundations.* San Francisco, CA: Jossey-Bass Publishers, Inc., 1998.

On Etiquette:

1. Fox, Sue. *Etiquette for Dummies.* 2000. Forest City, CA: IDG Books Worldwide, Inc., 2001.

2. Ford, Charlotte. *Charlotte Ford's Guide to Manners for the Modern Age.* New York City, NY: Crown Publishers, 2000.

About the Co-authors

Charles M. Dobbs has 25 years of experience as a faculty member and college administrator at several institutions. Over the years, he has worked in strategic planning, institutional assessment, and marketing, grantsmanship, professional development, student recruitment and retention, international studies, and fundraising. He has served on many panels assessing grant proposals. He also has served as a consultant to community colleges, private colleges, and non-profit organizations. Dr. Dobbs has given many grantsmanship seminars. He is a professor of history and assistant to the president at Iowa State University.

Robert J. Ligouri is President of the Oxford Group, Inc. Previously he was Vice President of Development for West Des Moines Dowling High in Iowa and, among other accomplishments, oversaw a capital campaign that raised millions of dollars over five years. Before that, he spent ten years as Executive Director of Special Olympics of Iowa where he oversaw an expansion in fundraising, budget, clients served, etc. In both of these positions, he built volunteer organizations, organized major fund raising drives, and secured funds for expanding programs and services. And, for more than fifteen years, he has been writing business and strategic plans for clients.

Printed in the United States
23764LVS00001B/438